FUTURE TENSE

HOW WE MADE
ARTIFICIAL INTELLIGENCE—
AND HOW IT WILL
CHANGE EVERYTHING

ALSO BY MARTHA BROCKENBROUGH

Alexander Hamilton, Revolutionary
Unpresidented

FUTURE TENSE

HOW WE MADE
ARTIFICIAL INTELLIGENCE—
AND HOW IT WILL
CHANGE EVERYTHING

MARTHA BROCKENBROUGH

FEIWEL AND FRIENDS
New York

NOTE TO READERS
As of press time, the URLs displayed in this book link or refer to existing sites. The publisher and author are not responsible for any content that appears on third-party websites and the publisher is not responsible for any content that appears on, or is produced by, websites and organizations with which the author is affiliated.

A Feiwel and Friends Book
An imprint of Macmillan Publishing Group, LLC
120 Broadway, New York, NY 10271 • fiercereads.com

Our books may be purchased in bulk for promotional, educational, or business use. Please contact your local bookseller or the Macmillan Corporate and Premium Sales Department at (800) 221-7945 ext. 5442 or by email at MacmillanSpecialMarkets@macmillan.com.

Library of Congress Cataloging-in-Publication Data
Names: Brockenbrough, Martha, author.
Title: Future tense : how we made Artificial Intelligence-and how it will change everything / Martha Brockenbrough.
Description: First edition. | New York : Feiwel and Friends [2024] | Includes bibliographical references and index. | Audience: Ages 12 and up | Audience: Grades 10–12 | Summary: "In this nonfiction book for teens, readers are guided through the development of this world-changing technology, exploring how AI has touched every corner of our world, including education, healthcare, work, politics, war, international relations, and even romance. This is essential reading for anyone who wants to understand how artificial intelligence got here, how to make the best use of it, and how we can expect it to transform our lives"— Provided by publisher.
Identifiers: LCCN 2023028595 | ISBN 9781250765925 (hardcover)
Subjects: LCSH: Artificial intelligence—Forecasting—Juvenile literature. | Artificial intelligence—Social aspects—Juvenile literature.
Classification: LCC Q335.4 .B76 2024 | DDC 006.3—dc23/eng/20231130
LC record available at https://lccn.loc.gov/2023028595

First edition, 2024
Book design by Ellen Duda and Mallory Grigg
Feiwel and Friends logo designed by Filomena Tuosto

Printed in the United States of America

ISBN 978-1-250-76592-5

10 9 8 7 6 5 4 3 2 1

To my dogs:
I hope our robot overlords love human beings
as much as I love you.[1]

(And all right, fine. Also to my cats, even though
they sometimes make it very hard to type.)

Foreword

The future is not what you think.

You can read this sentence in two ways.

It *could* mean that your predictions about the future are incorrect. We don't have the flying cars that Henry Ford assured us we'd have all the way back in 1940, for example.

But it could also mean that future will not be determined by what *you* think, but rather by what someone else—or some*thing* else—thinks.

This book is about both meanings.

All technology changes the world. Artificial intelligence will change the world more than nearly any other technology that's come before. It will transform the way we live, learn, and work.

Part of this transformation has begun.

Things that felt out of reach a decade ago, like human-level speech recognition, have been achieved for certain languages and dialects. Being able to chat with a bot like Siri or Alexa is so common now we don't even think twice about what a marvel it is.

Not every change will be as easy to get used to.

AI is going to affect kids at school. Adults at work. It will play a role in keeping you healthy . . . in national security, ranging from everything from espionage to war . . . in our relationships with each other . . . and even what it means to be alive.

That's why it's vital to understand where AI came from, how it works, how you both affect and are affected by it, and how you—and your fellow human beings—can thrive in an increasingly automated world.

We already know that someday, in some contexts, AI will far surpass human intelligence. How we prepare and respond when that day comes will make all the difference for our species and even the planet.

That's what this book aims to do—help you understand this technology's origins, its potential, and the role you have in making sure it's used for good.

PART I

I

IN THE BEGINNING, THERE WERE HUMAN BRAINS

Everything is theoretically impossible, until it's done.[2]
–Robert Heinlein

‖‖‖‖‖‖‖‖‖‖‖‖‖‖‖‖‖‖‖‖‖‖‖‖‖‖‖‖‖

Chapter One

What's AI, Anyway?

Before we can understand how our future with artificial intelligence will look, we have to know what artificial intelligence is—and what it isn't.

To do *that*, we need a definition of *intelligence*. This is the funny part: Not even experts on intelligence agree on a definition of the word.

For now, it's enough to say that intelligence is the ability to learn—and then to apply that knowledge to a goal.

The goal part is important. A piece of paper might have facts written on it, but it's never going to do anything with them all by itself. Paper is a tool, but it's not intelligent. It doesn't observe the world and react to it. Intelligent beings do.

We used to think humans were the only intelligent species. That's not true, though. Plenty of animals and even some plants meet this definition of intelligence.[3] And now, certain machines meet the definition, too.

It's important to remember that AI is code that's written—usually but not always by people—to perform certain kinds of tasks. AI is in use when machines take data, learn from it, and apply the learning to a task. It's fun to joke about our future evil robot overlords, but that's not what we're talking about. Not yet, anyway.

We're also not talking about the kinds of robots you often see in factories, the kind blamed for job loss through automation. It's true that many jobs have vanished this way. But a robot in a factory is not necessarily AI. If it can't learn and instead repeats the same task, it's missing the *intelligence* part of the AI equation.

AI doesn't even need to have a robot-like body. If you have a smartphone in your pocket, then you're walking around with AI.

For now, think of AI as falling into two buckets: narrow and general.

◀ ■ ▶

Narrow artificial intelligence already exists.

If you've been online, you have almost certainly encountered narrow AI. If you've ever asked Amazon's Alexa, Microsoft's Cortana, Samsung's Bixby, or Apple's Siri anything, you've interacted with artificial intelligence. Also, social media apps like TikTok use AI to serve up posts designed to give you a certain experience.

That sounds like kind of a squishy way to describe it, doesn't it? "A certain experience."

But that's really what it is. The type of experience you get is one determined by TikTok's strategies. If they want you to stay online, they can adjust it to keep you riveted based on what you do when you use it. It's even possible for social media apps to change your emotional state without your knowledge. Their software, guided by algorithms that let it learn from you and others, can influence your behavior and your feelings.

This is what narrow AI does well: It lets computers strive toward goals based on rules it has discovered through trial and error.

Not all computer programs are AI. Plenty of software is rules-based, which means someone has created a list of commands for the program to follow. A web page built in HTML is an example of this. It is made using tags that don't change, and it's the same page every time.

In contrast, AI uses large amounts of data, and by trial and error, discovers rules and patterns on its own. Another expression for this is *machine learning*, a branch of AI that involves learning from data, usually by updating some parameters that can be fine-tuned. Most modern AI involves machine learning.

The goal can be varied: selling socks on Instagram, catching a bogus credit card transaction, detecting disease, writing Shakespearean-style sonnets, or creating faces that look exactly like real people. The results are getting better all the time. A few years ago, for example, AI-generated cat faces were creatures of true horror; ones produced by new algorithms are excellent.

◀ ■ ▶

Artificial general intelligence (AGI) does not exist yet.

That's the kind of broad intelligence that human beings have—and then some. A machine with artificial general intelligence could achieve *any* complex goal, regardless of training or environment. While it's tempting to say "anything a human can do intellectually," this is not likely to be the case. Today's narrow AI is built as an echo of the human brain. But there's no guarantee that AGI will have intelligence that is similar to the kind people have. Eventually, if a model for AGI emerges, many experts believe it will surpass what human beings can do with our brains. (And naturally, other experts don't—but if the success of machine learning with games is any indication, the abilities of future algorithms will astonish us.)

Experts haven't decided whether a machine with artificial general intelligence would have consciousness. Defining consciousness is a hard problem. To simplify things for now, we can consider that something has consciousness if it's aware of itself and its experience in the world. Whether it has consciousness or not, AI will someday beat human intelligence at every single cognitive task—kind of like the way you can read, write, and do math in a way that cats and dogs can't. (This is not to say that cats and dogs can't do math; they can! But humans do have larger brains capable of more sophisticated things.)

For now, though, think about AI as either narrow or general. Narrow AI is already influencing your life. The other might someday—but not in the immediate future.

◀ ■ ▶

AI is already pervasive. If you were very young or not even born in 2012, when something called *deep neural networks* took off, it can be hard to realize how much this is the case.

Whether or not you've always lived with it, machine learning is everywhere now, both online and off—and it's not always easy to tell when you're seeing it.

Unlike a piece of hardware, like an iPad, a neural network is made of lines of code that you can't see. But it's probably something you interact with daily.

Let's say you have a smartphone. If you unlock it with your fingerprint or face, then you're using AI. This same kind of facial recognition is sometimes used at airports for international travel. Law enforcement agencies also use it.

It's all over social media, too. Every time an app suggests you tag a photo of yourself or someone you know, it's using this technology to recognize faces (and that is controversial, as you'll soon learn).

Your phone might also come with a built-in bot. These bots can shop for you, tell jokes, play music, give directions, place calls, and answer questions—all prompted by the sound of your voice and processed by AI.

Let's say you're writing a paper or sending a text. That means you know how hard it is to duck autocorrect. Its cousin, autocomplete, uses a kind of AI to anticipate what you plan to write next. Search engines use data from other users' queries to help you find what you're looking for (this is why the suggested queries are sometimes weird and even offensive).

| 🔍 | will artificial intelligence| | ✕ | 🔍 |

🔍   will artificial intelligence **take over**

🔍   will artificial intelligence **take over the world**

🔍   will artificial intelligence **take away jobs**

🔍   will artificial intelligence **replace humans**

🔍   will artificial intelligence **surpass human intelligence**

🔍   will artificial intelligence **and human creativity**

🔍   will artificial intelligence **take over jobs**

🔍   will artificial intelligence **replace doctors**

🔍   will artificial intelligence **destroy humanity**

🔍   will artificial intelligence **replace human intellectual work**

Report inappropriate predictions

Google tries to predict your query using the data from other people's searches. (Google)

◀ ■ ▶

Maybe you're watching videos on YouTube or looking at photos on Instagram. The recommendations are generated by AI. The same is true for the ads for sneakers and clothes that appear in your feed.

Social media networks and apps also sometimes use AI to make sure users aren't bullying others or making posts with inappropriate language. (They also sometimes use human beings for this.)

AI bots can converse—sometimes so well you won't even know you're talking to a computer.

And AI systems can write, create music, and make pictures good enough to fool people into thinking that human beings made them.

But it's not just online and in devices.

AI can drive cars and trucks. Fully autonomous cars aren't widely available yet, but ones

A conversation between the author and her Replika chat bot. (Martha Brockenbrough)

that partner with human beings are. Robots with AI can pick up and sort packages—a surprisingly tricky task for nonhumans. In hospitals, robots can deliver medicines, relieving overworked humans from that chore and even preventing human error.

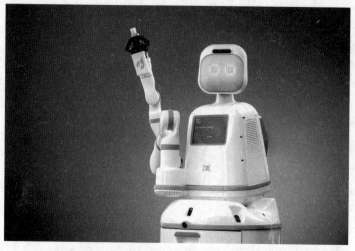

Moxi, a robot built by Diligent Robotics, helps hospital staff complete routine chores all on its own. (Diligent Robotics)

Drones are being used to find lost people, and some of those are trained to find the sounds of screaming humans, which seems horrifying until you remember tales of people being buried under rubble.

In short, there are tons of places where artificial intelligence will be used and where it will be useful. In the near future, you can expect AI to affect your education, your health and fitness, your travels, your finances, what you buy, click, and watch, and maybe even your relationships. It has the potential to remake economies and influence world politics, including causing diplomatic failures that lead to war and other forms of violence.

You can be certain that it's going to change modern life the way the internet did—and then some. The more you know about it, the better prepared you'll be for a future that is unlike anything humanity has yet experienced.

CHAPTER TWO

The Long Human Quest for AI

AI seems modern. Maybe even futuristic. But it's actually an ancient idea that we made real through a combination of vision, invention, insight, and perseverance.

How old is the idea? A centuries-old Chinese text describes an automaton built in 1000 BC by an engineer named Yan Shi. It could move and even sing perfectly in tune. Ancient Egyptians imagined statues brought to life with captured souls.

Later, the Greeks imagined that Hephaestus, their god of fire, built a huge bronze automaton named Talos. Powered by a vein of magical blood, Talos had one job: to keep the island of Crete safe by flinging boulders at enemies or superheating himself to scorch pirates. That wasn't all. Hephaestus, who had a disabled leg, also made a set of wheeled tripods to help him move— arguably history's first imagined version of a self-driving car.

Here's Talos keeping Crete safe in *Attack of the Titans*. (Columbia Pictures)

That's what all technology does: makes it easier to do what we need, whether that is military defense or a mobility aid—or even help with math.

You might have played with an abacus in elementary school, for example. If you added and subtracted with those sliding beads, you've used a tool that's more than 2,600 years old. At least 2,000 years ago, someone invented a device with 37 bronze gears that could track the movements of the moon and sun. It could also predict eclipses. More than 1,200 years ago, Aztecs invented a tool called a nepōhualtzintzin, which calculated numbers and planetary movements using beads and string. Users wore it on their wrists.

The suanpan is a Chinese abacus. *Calculate* comes from *calculus*, the Latin word for a pebble used in an abacus. (David R. Tribble)

These devices aren't AI in the way that a computer scientist today would define it. But they are part of the ancient human tradition of invention, saving or enhancing human labor and reducing human error. To some people, that's a basic definition of artificial intelligence: a tool that helps people with their thinking. But there's more to it. These inventions, imagined and real, can be seen to come from a desire to lift humanity out of oppression and struggle.

The Greek philosopher Aristotle observed this more than 2,300 years ago: "There is only one condition in which we can imagine managers not needing subordinates and masters not needing slaves. This condition would be that each instrument could do its own work, at the word of command or by intelligent anticipation."

Imagining tools that do their own work on command—or even by anticipating a command—sounds exactly like the aims of artificial intelligence today. (It should be noted, though, that Aristotle didn't oppose enslaving humans.)

Aristotle imagined something like AI 2,300 years ago. (Jastrow, Ludovisi Collection)

◄ ■ ►

First, we had to figure out how to think.

The world didn't come with an instruction manual. Even so, people have done a remarkably good job discerning its unwritten laws. This is exactly what programmers design AI to do: figure out through trial and error how to get a desired result.

If you've ever played a video game like *SimCity*, you've done this discerning yourself. To play, you have to track a bunch of interconnected variables and make decisions accordingly. This forces you to figure out the underlying rules that govern the game.

For example, if you want to increase your population, you have to build more houses. But if you build them too quickly, you'll deplete the forest . . . All of this requires thinking and the formulation of theories about the rules of the world. You win—or at least do well—when you figure out the hidden logic.

Human beings didn't evolve knowing how to think about big, abstract problems in a formal way. We first had to conceive of logic. Aristotle's description of the framework for it has been particularly influential, even with the kind of thinking that gave rise to computers and software.

Using Aristotelian logic, you make conclusions using syllogisms. A syllogism starts with two premises that overlap:

- **All pies are round.**
- **All round food is delicious** (e.g., pizza, donuts, and quesadillas).

Then you make a conclusion based on the premises:

Therefore, pies are delicious.

This approach doesn't guarantee that the underlying premises are correct. You might hate pizza, and it is also possible to bake a rectangular pie. But the syllogism gives us a way to describe and understand the world, a way of knowing things. It's also a way of abstracting general rules for categorizations. If we hadn't developed this logic, we wouldn't have digital devices.

Muhammad ibn Musa al-Khwarizmi, as featured on a Soviet postage stamp.

George Boole invented Boolean algebra.

AI uses algorithms that offer up a set of rules. The word *algorithm* has ancient origins. It comes from the last name of a Persian scholar named Muhammad ibn Musa al-Khwarizmi, who invented algebra around 825.

Another critical transformation in the history of thought came about in the 1800s, when an English math professor named George Boole invented a system using three words to figure out whether something was true or false.

In describing this method—which is now called Boolean logic—Boole's goal was to figure out how human minds work.[4] Later, it turned out to have huge implications for creating artificial intelligence.

How Boolean Logic Determines Whether Something Is True or False with Three Little Words

The three words AND, OR, and NOT are known as *operators*.

If something meets the conditions of the operator, then it is true. If it doesn't, then it is false.

You might have used these operators with a search engine to limit your results—for example, to find web pages that have clowns AND snakes. Or clowns OR snakes. Or clowns, but NOT snakes. The search engine gives you whatever results would make the query true.

◀ ■ ▶

After logic, we needed computers.

Logic itself wasn't enough. We also needed to invent computers—both the hardware and the software. A funny fact: *Computer* is a word that originally described people who were good at math. These human computers were usually women, because the work was not prestigious and the people who did it could be paid less. That means that the first human-made computers were "artificial computers."

These early computing devices were analog, meaning they ran with cranks and gears instead of software. The first of these was built by a rich English tinkerer named Charles Babbage, who loved math. Back then, people solving difficult equations used books with tables of calculations already done. This was useful—except when there were mistakes due to human error. People needed reliable numbers for many things: banking, construction, navigation, insurance, finance, and astronomy. If you used the wrong number

Charles Babbage built the first analog computer.

when you were trying to chart a course for a ship, for example, people could die.

In 1822, Babbage designed a model for a large, crank-operated device with gears, ratchets, and rods, which he called a Difference Engine. It solved equations, and it quickly generated accurate tables of numbers. Then Babbage drew up plans for the Analytical Engine, which could do even more things. Programs would be set with punch cards, and it also had memory—essentially an analog computer with a stored memory and a central processing unit. Babbage thought people would use his Analytical Engine for mathematical calculations, but a brilliant 17-year-old mathematician named Ada Lovelace saw more potential.

Ada Lovelace wrote the first computer program, inspired by the plans for a device she saw when she was a teenager.
(Antoine Claudet, reproduction by Geoffrey Bond)

This Analytical Engine was the first fully automated counting machine. (John Cummings)

She correctly theorized that the machine could be used to write music and more. A decade after she first saw the plans for the engine, she translated an article about the device from French to English, and in her footnotes was a sequence of operations that some people view as the first software ever written.

Babbage never got this Analytical Engine fully built, but in 2002, the Science Museum in London followed Babbage's instructions, and the machine actually worked.

Babbage wasn't the only person to understand that people could build machines to do intellectual work. In 1873, William Thompson, the future Lord Kelvin, made an analog tide predictor that could simultaneously process the many factors that influence tides.

In 1931, a professor at the Massachusetts Institute of Technology (MIT) named Vannevar[5] Bush and two of his graduate students built an analog computer that could do calculus. It was cool, but there was a problem: The wheels and discs that performed the calculations had to be reassembled every time someone wanted to solve a different problem.

One of Bush's students fixed that—and more.

The student, Claude Shannon, grew up tinkering. As a boy, he built a

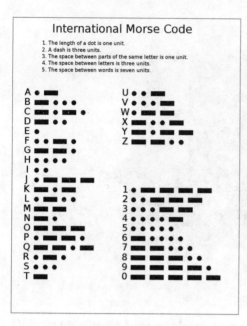

International Morse Code

1. The length of a dot is one unit.
2. A dash is three units.
3. The space between parts of the same letter is one unit.
4. The space between letters is three units.
5. The space between words is seven units.

A • ▬	U • • ▬
B ▬ • • •	V • • • ▬
C ▬ • ▬ •	W • ▬ ▬
D ▬ • •	X ▬ • • ▬
E •	Y ▬ • ▬ ▬
F • • ▬ •	Z ▬ ▬ • •
G ▬ ▬ •	
H • • • •	
I • •	
J • ▬ ▬ ▬	
K ▬ • ▬	1 • ▬ ▬ ▬ ▬
L • ▬ • •	2 • • ▬ ▬ ▬
M ▬ ▬	3 • • • ▬ ▬
N ▬ •	4 • • • • ▬
O ▬ ▬ ▬	5 • • • • •
P • ▬ ▬ •	6 ▬ • • • •
Q ▬ ▬ • ▬	7 ▬ ▬ • • •
R • ▬ •	8 ▬ ▬ ▬ • •
S • • •	9 ▬ ▬ ▬ ▬ •
T ▬	0 ▬ ▬ ▬ ▬ ▬

The Morse code alphabet.
(Rhey T. Snodgrass and Victor F. Camp)

telegraph between his farm and the one next door, where his friend Rodney lived. Shannon became an expert in Morse code, which uses dots and dashes—a binary system—to send messages. By the time he studied math and electrical engineering at the University of Michigan, binary code was second nature.

After graduation, he got a summer job designing telephone circuits at Bell Labs. At the time, telephone circuits were designed by trial and error, a slow and expensive process. Shannon saw a new way of doing things. Circuits can be either on or off, he understood. These two states are binary—like the true or false of Boolean logic. When Shannon had that insight, he realized that he could design phone routing circuits using Boolean algebra. Later, this same idea worked as the basis for the design of digital circuits for computers. The master's thesis he wrote when studying with Vannevar Bush is considered by many to be the most important of the 20th century.

Meanwhile, a young English mathematician named Alan Turing imagined another sort of device that could run multiple programs at once, pairing hardware with

Claude Shannon invented information theory, ushering in the digital age. (Konrad Jacobs)

16

software—exactly how computers run today. He eventually designed abstract models for several "Turing machines," each capable of running a program. His goal was to make a universal machine that could run any program, and he fully expected machine intelligence to someday be indistinguishable from human. In 1950, Turing wrote a paper describing something he called "the imitation game," now known as the Turing test. A machine passes the test if it can display intelligence well enough that an observer can't tell the difference between the computer and a human competitor.

By the time Turing came up with his Turing test, modern computers had been around for five years. An engineer and mathematician named John von Neumann wrote a report capturing the first computer architecture. Under his system, computers had an internal processor and memory that held both their programs and data. They also had external storage and devices for getting information in and data out. Computers today have all of this—a unit for processing, memory and hard drives, keyboards, and monitors.

Back then, though, we didn't understand how information could be digitized.

But Claude Shannon, the Morse code whiz, figured that out, too. Working at Bell Labs with the superstar researchers[6] there, Shannon published a paper called "A Mathematical Theory of Communication" in 1948.

Before this landmark paper, communicating over long distances could be difficult. We'd tried many things: messengers, smoke signals, carrier pigeons, postal services, telegraphs, radios, telephones, television, and fax technology. Some methods were too slow. The faster methods were subject to *noise*—unwanted signals that interfere with the important ones. Radio was transmitted along AM and FM frequencies, for example, and it got staticky.

You can refine the technologies to make them work better—building bigger broadcast towers, for example. But that kind of improvement only gets you so far, because the noise remains. You can't just boost the signal to make it louder, because that boost also increases the noise.

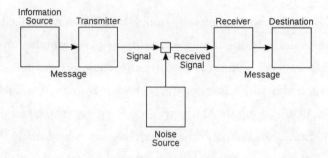

Claude Shannon's model of how all communication works. (Wanderingstan at English Wikipedia)

Shannon took a step back from the existing engineering methods and asked if there was a unifying factor for all kinds of communication that could be expressed mathematically. In his paper, he modeled what communication looks like. Here's how he broke it down.

1. A source of information creates a message.
2. A transmitter encodes it so that it can be sent as a signal.
3. It goes through a channel.
4. Noise gums things up.
5. A receiver decodes the message.
6. The message arrives at a destination, which could be a person or a device—or even something as tiny as a cell.

The model is simple, and that's its strength. This theory describes how a telephone call works. But it also describes how a letter might be sent through the mail. It even captures how DNA sends instructions to an organism. Shannon showed that *all* communication—information transfer—follows this pattern.

After Shannon transformed communication into an abstract concept, he could apply probability principles to it. Communication is in many ways *predictable*. For example, if you read *the clown juggled three b___*, you can most likely figure out that the incomplete word is *balls*. It's probable, even though the clown could be juggling three babies. What predictability means is that some letters and some words are more likely to appear next to each other than others. But that's not all. Y cn prbly ls rd ths sntnc vn thgh t dsn't hv ny vwls.

That you can figure out these things indicates something important. Communication is redundant. The redundancy helps ensure our messages get through. We also sometimes add redundancy when we want to make sure the signal is really clear. When people spell their names on the phone—"*S* as in *star*, *A* as in *apple*, *M* as in *monster*"—that's a way of adding redundancy and increasing the likelihood of successful transmission. But you can also reduce redundancy. Abbreviations are an example of this.

Redundancy means that communication is predictable to a certain extent. If language wasn't predictable, for example, then every letter would have the same frequency of being used. But we know that some letters in English are more common than others. You're more likely to encounter an *E* than you are a *Q*. When Samuel Morse invented Morse code, he made *E* a single dot, knowing that it was important to make a frequently occurring letter easy to transmit. The rarely used *Q*, on the other hand, is dash-dash-dot-dash. We also know that some words are more likely to be paired than others. *The* is almost never followed by *this*, but is often followed by *end*.

How much uncertainty is there with messages? This is what Shannon needed to calculate. He called this uncertainty *entropy*. To come up with a mathematical model for entropy, Shannon needed something to measure it. He called that unit of measure a *bit*, which is short for *binary digit*.

Building on his work with circuit design, he said a bit could be either a 1 or a 0. If you could encode information using 1s and 0s, you could essentially reduce its size without distorting or losing the meaning. If you could make a message small enough, you could escape the problem of noise.

This was important because of the way messages travel. Messages are sent through channels the way milk travels through a straw. Channels have capacities, sort of like different straws have different widths. You can't fit a bowling ball through a drinking straw, for example. But imagine you could compress the bowling ball by breaking it into bits and reassembling them later. Calculating the uncertainty of a message is key to compressing it to fit whatever channel it's traveling. As long as the channel capacity is greater than the flow of communication, the message will be received.

This changed the game of communications. Instead of boosting signals and having to put up with boosted noise, Shannon came up with a way of fitting bowling balls through straws.

His binary digital communication theory launched a whole new academic discipline called Information Theory. This led to the internet, which revolutionized human communication and connection—everything from text messages, photos, audio, video, and even deep-space probes relaying videos and other data back from Mars.

◀ ■ ▶

Alan Turing Helped Defeat Nazi Germany

Alan Turing's work became critically important in 1939, when the British declared war on Nazi Germany.

The German navy used codes that many considered unbreakable to communicate. Their device, called an Enigma, scrambled letters that were typed on a keyboard with a series of rotors, spitting out an encrypted message, giving the Germans a decided military advantage—enough to win the war.

An Enigma machine, which the Nazis used to send coded messages in World War II. Their use of *Heil Hitler* in every message enabled Alan Turing and team to crack the code. (Daderot)

To beat the Nazis, the Allies had to crack this code. But it wasn't going to be easy. There were almost 159 quintillion settings on an Enigma. No one could possibly guess which one had been used, and the Nazis switched settings every time the clock struck midnight.

Polish scientists had already created a manual device, called a Bomba, which was good at cracking codes. But in 1939 the Germans introduced more

Alan Turing cracked the Nazi Enigma code, helping end World War II.

rotors that made their codes too complex for a Bomba to beat by the midnight deadline. Turing built an electric machine that was faster. He also discovered a flaw in the Nazi encryption code: A letter was never encrypted as itself. This feature narrowed the possibilities substantially.

Then Turing guessed correctly that every message would contain the words *Heil Hitler,* and, using that pattern and a diagonal plugboard created by Turing's teammate Gordon Welchman, he broke the Nazi code and helped bring about the Germans' defeat.

After the war, he continued his work, becoming instrumental in the development of early computer hardware and software—essentially launching the computer science field. He became the director of the computing laboratory at the University of Manchester.

Despite his heroic contributions to World War II, Turing's life ended tragically. He was arrested in 1952 for having sexual relationships with men, which was illegal at the time in the United Kingdom. Sentenced to chemical castration and barred from the security clearance he needed to do the work he loved, Turing died by suicide. But he fully expected the work to be carried on and artificial intelligence to become a reality before the 20th century ended.

By then, he predicted, "one will be able to speak of machines thinking without expecting to be contradicted."[7]

◀ ■ ▶

This sentence was encrypted by the Enigma cipher:

HQVHGYYRCHVMCYRVWLPSMBJKMJAVNLQMJWVQZVRMW

(It says, "This sentence was encrypted by the Enigma cipher.")

||||||||||||||||||||||||||||||

Chapter Three

Excitement and Inhibition

As Claude Shannon worked on his paper establishing information theory, others made progress in understanding the human brain, which contains billions of cells called neurons. AI today works with its own version of neurons.

In 1943, two years after Alan Turing's team cracked the Enigma cipher, neurophysiologist Warren McCulloch and a logician named Walter Pitts wrote a paper that inspired the first artificial neuron.

Think of a neuron like a box with a lightbulb on it. This hypothetical box requires a certain amount of data to fill it. If you put in enough data, the bulb lights up. But if the data doesn't hit that threshold, the bulb stays dark. This is binary, like true or false, on or off.

Your brain has 100 billion neurons making electrical connections all the time. An artificial neural network is simpler, and this first one was the simplest.

Their model is a *one-layer network*—one level where calculations occur—in addition to an input layer (g) and an output layer (f).

The input layer has multiple Xs—things you can input. If you look at the output layer, you can see that it is binary—the answer is either 0 or 1, no or yes, based on how the inputs are crunched.

There are several *excitatory* inputs. These make the neuron fire once their combined value hits a certain threshold. You can think of them as a series of on switches. There is also an *inhibitory* input. This prevents the neuron from firing if the number doesn't hit the threshold—sort of like filling our hypothetical box. These are the off switches.

How's this work? Let's say you are trying to predict whether your cat will sit on your lap.

You might consider several inputs:

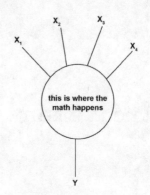

this is where the math happens

1. Input the Xes.
2. Perform the calculations.
3. The neuron is either excited or not—it's excited when the result of the calculation is above a certain threshold.

This first artificial neuron performs calculations on one layer. (Whiteknight at English Wikibooks)

1. X1: Your lap is in a sunbeam.
2. X2: You are wearing jeans, which your cat likes.
3. X3: It's your cat's regular snuggle time.
4. X4: You really want your cat to sit on your lap.

The inputs either excite the neuron or don't. For example, your cat likes sunbeams and jeans. Those *excite* the neuron. But cats, who can be jerks, don't want to do what you want them to do. Your desire for your cat to sit on your lap *inhibits* the neuron.

The mathematical function the neuron performs considers all of the inputs and then gives a yes or no answer.

This artificial neuron was flexible enough to show results for a variety of Boolean functions, but it had its limits. You couldn't weight inputs differently—for example, your cat's love of jeans is *less* than its hatred of doing something you want it to do—so the predictions were not as reliable as they could have been.

But it was still an exciting leap forward.

◄ ■ ►

Developments like this made people look to the future with hope and high expectations. In 1950, Claude Shannon wrote in *Scientific American* about chess-playing computers that "it is certainly plausible to me that in a few decades machines will be beyond humans."

Shannon took it for granted that someday, computers *would* be able to think. He said, "I'm a machine and you're a machine, and we both think, don't we?"[8]

The 1950s were an important time in the history of AI. In 1954, a machine managed to translate from Russian to English using syntactical analysis and a dictionary with 250 words in it. The next year, a coder named Arthur Samuel wrote a program that could play checkers. Late in the summer of 1955, several researchers decided to plan a project on the Dartmouth campus.

The big idea: Assemble a team to explore whether machines could emulate human intelligence. At first, 10 men were invited. But eventually the group expanded to 20—all of them white. It's significant that women weren't included. In the 1940s, coding and operating computers was seen as women's work. But as the potential for computing became clear, men edged the women out.

In the summer of 1956, they gathered to study a variety of aspects of AI, including how a computer could be programmed to use a language, how to arrange neurons to form concepts, how to get a computer to improve itself, and even how to explore the role of randomness that enlivens creative thinking (as opposed to mere competent thinking, which is more formulaic). The men expected big progress in at least one of these areas. In retrospect, this optimism was premature.

For one thing, it was hard to understand and even define what artificial intelligence was. What's more, they weren't well organized. Some, like Shannon, couldn't stay the whole time. They also couldn't agree on important standards for the new field. Plus, they were competitive. Some participants, for example, had already written a program called Logic Theorist. It was the first to solve problems in a human-like way. It should have been exciting to the group, but their rivalries got in the way. One of its creators, Herbert Simon, later said, "They didn't want to hear from us, and we sure didn't want to hear from them: we had something to show them!"[9]

But it wasn't all human foibles holding AI back. Computers then were primitive. Until 1949, digital ones couldn't store commands. This meant these early computers could run programs, but they couldn't remember them. Computers also cost a fortune—$200,000 a month to lease. That's more than $2.4 million dollars today. Even if a university had the money, no one wanted to gamble so much cash on something unproven.

Still, there was one thing everyone agreed on in those days, despite the obstacles: We were going to figure out artificial intelligence.

In 1958—the year LEGO was patented in Denmark, the US launched its first satellite, and both instant noodles and NASA were created—we took another big leap forward.

Frank Rosenblatt tweaked the McCulloch-Pitts neuron and invented a machine called the Mark I Perceptron for the US Navy. His adjustments let him train the neuron to improve at tasks, one of which was to recognize triangles.

The $2 million machine (nearly $21 million today) had a camera and 400 photocells arranged in a grid that could make a 400-pixel image. The idea was to train the Perceptron to recognize a triangle. Once trained, it would turn on a light if it found a triangle shape in the 400 pixels. If it found another shape instead, the bulb stayed dark.

Rosenblatt's camera scanned ink and paper and sent data to the Perceptron. At first, the Perceptron made guesses. But Rosenblatt trained it using YES and NO buttons. The YES button didn't change any weights.

But the NO button prompted the machine to adjust its thresholds, making it more likely to get the right answer. The machine learned, and Rosenblatt had proved it. And it could learn to do more than tell a triangle from a circle.

Developers thought they'd have it reading and writing within a year, but as with many predictions related to AI, it didn't happen. Still, it was the first time an artificial neuron demonstrated the ability to learn—very much like a human brain.

NEW NAVY DEVICE LEARNS BY DOING

Psychologist Shows Embryo of Computer Designed to Read and Grow Wiser

WASHINGTON, July 7 (UPI) —The Navy revealed the embryo of an electronic computer today that it expects will be able to walk, talk, see, write, reproduce itself and be conscious of its existence.

The *New York Times* gave a breathless account of the Perceptron and its potential. (*New York Times*)

Between the mid-1950s and the mid-1970s, more progress happened. A federal defense program started funding the study of AI at universities. Computers also improved, as did the chips that ran them. During this era, many people thought human-level intelligence in computers was just around the corner.

In 1970, Marvin Minsky, a Dartmouth summer conference attendee, felt confident enough to tell *Life* magazine that in "three to eight years we will have a machine with the general intelligence of an average human being."[10]

But not long after Minsky's proclamation, an "AI Winter" set in—in part because Minsky himself wrote a book that made the Perceptron seem hopelessly limited. The Perceptron's single layer of neurons wasn't enough. But people hadn't yet figured out how to fix that. Nor had we built powerful enough computers.

An MIT professor named Hubert Dreyfus also criticized claims made by people in the field. And it turned out that early successes, like foreign language translations, were false starts. They could handle easy stuff, but not more difficult problems. A paper written for the British Science Research Council in 1973 said, essentially, that AI had been a dud, and the government agencies sponsoring the projects felt burned.

People had unrealistic expectations—huge progress actually had been made. But the disappointment led to reduced funding for more research. The technology that would someday be breakthrough—creating networks out of artificial neurons—was considered fringe, and people risked their careers and reputations pursuing it.

But one learning tool turned out to be surprisingly useful in the meantime: games.

||||||||||||||||||||||||||||||

CHAPTER FOUR

The Game Is Afoot

When you look at photographs of the founders of artificial intelligence, they look ready for a funeral. The men wear jackets and ties. Their hair is neatly combed.

Don't let that fool you. Many of them, Claude Shannon especially, liked to have fun. At the office, he rode his unicycle up and down the halls, sometimes while juggling. He built all sorts of gadgets: a trumpet that spewed fire; a number of unicycles, including one built for two; and a machine that did one thing after you pushed its ON button—use a mechanical hand to turn itself off. He also loved chess, and the game became part of AI history.

Games are great candidates for software and for AI algorithms because rules govern them, and the game ends when certain conditions are met. Games are one reason AI has progressed as far as it has.

Chess has long been associated with intelligence (and it should be equally associated with wealth, masculinity, and privilege). It's a strategy game, perfect for people with the cunning to see several steps ahead. There's no chance involved. Winning takes brainpower, and if you're trying to create artificial intelligence, chess is a natural challenge to take on.

In the late 1940s, Alan Turing and a mathematician named David Champernowne hashed out an algorithm for a computer chess program named Turochamp that could think two moves ahead. They couldn't get it running on an actual computer, but they used a printed version of the algorithm in a match against a friend in 1952. Each move was slow—it took about a half hour to manually check all the possible outcomes for two moves ahead. Turochamp lost after 29 moves.

Meanwhile, in 1950, Claude Shannon wrote a paper examining the many ways computer chess might be achieved. Among other things, the paper showed that the problem of computer chess wouldn't be solved by "brute force," meaning by listing all of the possibilities and then testing them. Chess had too many variations. He also wrote software that showed the world that computers could play, too. His computer really could make chess moves, but only the last ones in a game, when possible remaining moves decrease. Even so, this showed that computers could do more than make calculations; it could strategize with them.

Though the big dream for developers was always chess, checkers is a simpler challenge, so success here came first. In 1955, Arthur Samuel wrote a program that played checkers so well, it was featured on TV. This milestone meant a human being could create a system that could beat its programmer.

By 1990, computer checkers had gotten as good as the best human players in the world. An AI called Chinook took on the champion of the world, a man named Marion Tinsley, the greatest competitor in the history of the game. Because the rules forbid a machine from competing for a National Title, Tinsley actually retired from play to take on Chinook instead of human competitors. He'd lost only a few games in his life and craved the challenge.

Marion Tinsley, the best human checkers player ever. (Mark T. Foley)

The first time he faced Chinook, the computer made a bad tenth move. Tinsley knew it. "You're going to regret that."[11]

The computer resigned 26 moves later. Later, an analysis revealed that Tinsley had managed to see 64 moves into the future and had picked the single strategy that would have won the game—extraordinary for a human being.

Tinsley and Chinook faced off again in 1994. This time, human and machine tied six times. Tinsley withdrew because he wasn't feeling well. In the hospital the next day, an X-ray found a lump on his pancreas. Seven months later, cancer killed him.

The man who built Chinook, a University of Alberta professor named Jonathan Schaeffer, was haunted by Tinsley's death and the tie.[12] He worked doggedly to build a version of Chinook that could beat the one Tinsley faced. It took 13 years, but Schaeffer did it—and that's the version you can play online today.

◀ ■ ▶

Checkers isn't chess, though. Even with simple rules, chess is more complicated, precisely because there are so many ways the game can shift.

After each player moves the first time, there are 400 possible ways the game can go. After the second set of moves, that expands to 197,742. This becomes 121 million possibilities after just three moves. That number goes up until players once again reduce the possibilities with their moves. No one knows for sure how many possible chess games there are. But one computer science expert calculated there were more games than all the hairs on human heads, the grains of sand on Earth, and the atoms in the universe . . . multiplied by each other.[13]

For a human player, the more games you can memorize, the more strategies you can have. Becoming a grand master at chess requires fantastic feats of memory. According to one study, people who play at the top level have memorized about 100,000 opening moves.[14]

This is why a showdown between a human and a machine playing chess has always felt like a worthy test for AI developers. We know how to describe all the legal moves of the game, but it's tricky to write a single formula that determines the best move at any time.

In 1982, a Taiwanese student arrived at Carnegie Mellon with plans to build a chess-playing computer for his PhD dissertation. Feng-hsiung Hsu called his project ChipTest, and after he graduated in 1989, IBM Research hired him and a classmate to keep the project going. He joined the Deep Blue team, which set out to beat the youngest World Chess Champion in history, a Russian named Garry Kasparov. They set a match for February 10, 1996, in Philadelphia.

Kasparov had been playing chess since he was six. He'd been the world's top-ranking player since 1984, and he was a fierce competitor. As he put it, "professional chess is not a game, it is about killing someone across the board."[15]

For some observers, it wasn't so much a chess match as a portent for the future of human beings versus machines. Could one brilliant mind for chess murder a machine that could assess 50 billion chess positions in three minutes?

Kasparov was so sure he'd win, he wanted the $500,000 prize to be winner-take-all.

The day of the match was a mild one. No rain or snow and little wind, as if the city itself was holding its breath in anticipation. But that didn't last long. Kasparov lost the very first game. He came back to win the second game. The next three ended in draws. In game six, Deep Blue's last chance, Kasparov won. It was a decisive victory for the human being. Even so, the experience was eye-opening for Kasparov.

"I hardly believed before the match that there were so many things I could learn about the game of chess," Kasparov said.[16]

He agreed to a rematch in 1997, believing it would take until 2010 before a computer could beat him. He and Deep Blue met in New York City.

Kasparov started strong, winning the first game after 45 minutes. Then he lost his composure, missed a mistake Deep Blue made that could have led to a draw, and resigned. In the third game, he tried an unusual opening move but couldn't do more than tie.

Kasparov, rattled, suspected the IBM team was cheating, and he almost dropped out. But he hung in there through game five, where he and Deep Blue were tied at two-and-a-half games each.

Kasparov tried again to confuse Deep Blue with his opening. He didn't think the machine would understand that it needed to sacrifice a knight to keep in the game. But Hsu and the other developers had thought of that twist, and in the end, Kasparov lost.

It stunned the world, boosted IBM stock, and got more clicks online than the Atlanta Summer Olympics. Kasparov wanted a rematch, but IBM declined. The team had achieved its goal: It had developed a computer that could take down the champion of the world in a game that represented human intellect.

Afterward, Kasparov blamed his own emotions for the loss.

"I lost my fighting spirit," he said. Facing an opponent that felt cold, calculating, and relentless proved too much—even for the best human opponent in the world.[17]

Garry Kasparov lost control of his emotions–and then he lost to Deep Blue. (Owen Williams, Kasparov Agency)

CHAPTER FIVE

||||||||||||||||||||||||||||||||

The Power of Persistence

IBM's technology was impressive. Even so, Deep Blue doesn't meet everyone's definition of artificial intelligence. The developers analyzed thousands of chess master games and made parameters that Deep Blue used to pick the best move.

It took something else, the development of a neural network, to create the AI that we're familiar with today. When you link more than one artificial neuron, you have a neural network.

These neural networks didn't pop up like mushrooms in the woods. For many years, they were considered a lost cause. This is because people had come to understand serious limits of the Perceptron, the software modeled after a human neuron. Most people thought it was a waste of time to keep trying.

But not Geoffrey Hinton, a University of Toronto computer science professor. Despite the fact that his work was considered fringe, Hinton kept at it because he believed there was no other possibility than neural networks for AI.

"The brain has to work somehow," he said, "and neural networks are a simplified model of how the brain works."[18]

It was a hard slog for Hinton, who is a cognitive scientist, a computer scientist, and—coincidentally—a descendant of George Boole. The United Kingdom, where he was born, cut his funding. So he came to the United

States, but his only source of funding here was from the US military. He didn't want anything to do with the creation of weapons, so he left for Canada. From there, in 1986, he coauthored a breakthrough paper about a training technique for neural networks. Called *back propagation*, it's a way of improving the accuracy of neural networks that have more than one layer. The more layers a neural network has, the more powerful. These are known as deep networks, and Hinton's paper shared key insights for creating them, setting the stage for enormous progress.

Geoffrey Hinton never gave up on deep neural networks. (Eviatar Bach)

Hinton wasn't the only one who believed neural networks were the future of AI. A French-born computer scientist named Yann LeCun and another Canadian computer scientist, Yoshua Bengio, figured out how to use the technology to recognize handwriting in 1998.

Another stalwart was Fei-Fei Li, then an assistant professor at Princeton. She believed if algorithms had enough data to learn from, AI could succeed with image recognition. Li started work on a project called ImageNet in 2006. Her plan was to build a giant labeled database of images that developers could use to train their algorithms—the biggest ever made by far.

Like Hinton, Li was told she was wasting her time. Nonetheless, a colleague at Princeton, Christiane Fellbaum, had created a similar database called WordNet, which is like a thesaurus that links words according to their meaning and also labels the relationships of those meanings to each other. Li took the words in Fellbaum's WordNet database and used its features to create a huge database of images. Then she crowdsourced labels for each image.

There are problems with the database: It used images without permission and contained racist content. But it finally provided the trove of data needed to help machines recognize images. Starting in 2010, ImageNet ran a contest to see who could create algorithms that did the best job identifying which label most likely applied to the image. That first year, the winning entry got it right 47.1 percent of the time. Then, in 2012, Hinton's team entered something called AlexNet into the fray.

AlexNet is a deep convolutional neural network. *Deep* means many layers. *Convolutional* means that an image is broken into overlapping pieces. That technique gives an advantage—it means an object can appear anywhere in the image and still be understood by the network. So, if there's a lamb in the corner of a grassy field instead of the center, this neural network can still identify it.

AlexNet also had a secret weapon. The developer, Alex Krizhevsky, used graphics processing units called GPUs, typically used for video games, as he trained his neural network. These chips were more powerful than what had been used previously.

AlexNet clobbered the previous year's best performance, with an accuracy rate of almost 85 percent.[19] The runner-up was way behind, with less than 75 percent accuracy.

Fei-Fei Li put together an enormous bank of images that proved vital in training AI to recognize objects in photos. (ITU Pictures)

AlexNet works a lot like we imagine brains work. Let's say you're looking at a picture of a raccoon. Your eyes are sending data to your brain, where neurons detect the edges of the animal, light spots and dark spots, movement, and colors. Your brain processes each of those data points.

After that, your mind takes in texture, hair, skin, and finer information, all of which eventually fire the neurons that tell you what you're looking at. (Or what you *think* you're looking at, which you might revise with more data.)

Just as your brain learned how to recognize raccoons, AlexNet learned how to recognize features in images. Having a whole lot of data to look at was key. That plus the GPU for speedy processing, and many, many adjustments made by the developer using back propagation. The back propagation technique let Krizhevsky fine-tune the weights of the neural network. When developers tune the weights correctly, they reduce the error rate.

Krizhevsky's project touched off a revolution. After the debut of AlexNet, which had eight learnable layers, five of which were convolutional, deep convolutional neural networks flourished. Just four years later, Microsoft won the contest with one that had more than 100 layers, a sign of how rapidly the industry embraced the concept.

These deep learning systems are great at seeing patterns in data. And it's not just for images. It's also numbers, musical notes, and even styles of art.

One cool example of how it can be used is on display at the Rijksmuseum in Amsterdam. Rembrandt was a Dutch painter in the 1600s. His work can be worth hundreds of millions of dollars—but some of it has been damaged over time. A large painting called *The Night Watch* was trimmed to fit between the doors in Amsterdam's city hall. Using a copy of the painting that had been made before its unfortunate haircut, an AI mimicked the style and recreated what had been lost.[20]

AI helped replace the edges of this Rembrandt masterpiece after it had been cut down to fit through a door. (Alf van Beem)

Problems with WordNet and ImageNet

As exciting as giant datasets like WordNet and ImageNet seem, and as much as ImageNet helped push technology along, there are enormous problems with the content of both.

WordNet contains derogatory terms. When images are compiled based on those terms, they replicate the bigotry with image labels. Without the developers intending this, search results can entrench offensive and harmful stereotypes and biases.[21]

This is one of the biggest challenges the people developing these tools face: how to ensure the vast collections of data they're using for training are free from hateful content. In 2019, an art project called *ImageNet Roulette* showed systemic bias in the ImageNet collection. In response, ImageNet removed 600,000 photos.[22] It was the right thing to do, but it means that the systemic bias had been replicated for nine years. And ImageNet isn't the only trove of images based on WordNet.

It's a huge problem when datasets are biased. In 2020, after a Black man was wrongfully arrested based on facial recognition technology, Detroit's police chief said his department's tool failed 95 to 97 percent of the time.[23]

Moore's Law

In 1965, an engineer named Gordon Moore, who founded the microchip company Intel, observed that new computer chips tended to have double the transistors of their predecessors, giving them twice the power.

The observation came to be called Moore's Law—that computer chips would get twice as fast every year. In the 1970s, the speed increase in computer chips slowed slightly to double every two years, so Moore adjusted his law. Even so, the rapid improvement in chips meant better, faster computers for a remarkably long time.

It won't keep that pace forever, but for decades, Moore's Law has held true.

It's hard to visualize what exponential improvement looks like, but let's try: Say you had 500 people in your school in 1970. If the doubling-every-year version of Moore's Law applied to your school's enrollment, by 2022, your school would have had 2,251,799,813,685,248,000 students. That's more than 2.2 *quintillion* students, and a very crowded study hall. (The total would be 33,554,432,000 students if it took two years to double—a smaller number, but still crowded.)

At some point, making a chip smaller might end up costing more than it's worth. Moore's Law is slowing down, even as chip manufacturers find clever ways to squeeze more transistors into tiny chips.

But the end of Moore's Law might actually be a boon for artificial intelligence.

The futurist John Smart believes the end of Moore's Law will force engineers to stop improving AI from the top down and move toward letting machines take over their own development with deep learning.

"If you care about the development of artificial intelligence, you should pray for that prediction to be true," he said.[24]

But there's a risk, too, that a small number of companies with access to computing arrays and technical expertise will monopolize the power, influence, and capital that comes with it, which will not necessarily be good for humanity.

||||||||||||||||||||||||||||||||||

CHAPTER SIX

The Incredible Story
of AlphaGo

After deep convolutional neural networks captured the imagination of the AI world, people turned their attention to another game, one even more complicated than chess.

The game is called Go.

It's 4,000 years old—the world's oldest board game that's perpetually been played. In China, where it was invented, Go was considered one of the Four Arts that all Chinese nobility had to master, along with music, calligraphy, and painting.

Eventually, the game made its way to Korea and Japan, where, in the 17th century, it was such a big deal that competitive schools formed, and people started playing professionally.

Like chess, Go is a game of strategy. Also like chess, players use black or white pieces, but instead of chasing the king, players compete to capture territory.

To do this, you put your piece down on an intersection of the lines on the board. Black goes first, and white follows. The object is to trap your opponent's stones and capture territory. Whoever captures the most by the end of the game wins.

In some ways, Go is simpler than chess. The pieces are all the same size and shape. They don't move around the board. But it's also trickier. The board is larger, and there are more opening moves—361 compared to the 20 openings of chess.

Go requires both an overall strategy and smaller-scale tactics that support that strategy. This is why some people consider it the most complicated game in human history. Not only are there more possible configurations of a Go board than a chessboard, the game also has more possible variations than there are atoms in the universe. There isn't yet enough computer power to calculate every configuration.

People don't have enough brainpower to consider this many game variations. But the ones who do master Go have key skills. There's the ability to visualize the board a few moves ahead, and the ability to recognize patterns—what shapes can lead to good outcomes. There's mindset, too. Good players can take initiative, intimidate their opponents, and be creative about making sacrifices.

What would it take for a computer to compete?

A company called DeepMind decided to take on the challenge. If they could beat a world champion at the most complex board game, that would be huge.

Using a theory called temporal differences (TD) learning—which had been developed in part with a backgammon program in the 1990s—the DeepMind team fed the computer data from 100,000 games played by strong amateurs. TD learning is a type of reinforcement learning. This lets a neural network learn as it goes. Instead of waiting to collect a reward, a network estimates the reward it expects and then uses that estimate to update its parameters. In other words, it can use predictions to adjust along the way instead of waiting to learn at the conclusion of the game.

To help the software predict the best human moves, the team trained it using examples of good moves, a technique called supervised learning. Once the AI mastered the basics of play, they used reinforcement learning as the AI played against itself.

The idea was to train deep neural networks with a large set of data, and then let the algorithms continue to learn on their own. This was the major promise of this experiment with Go. The computer itself was doing what human beings could not do for it: use massive amounts of data to improve as a player.

This also is the key difference between AlphaGo and Deep Blue. Deep Blue was programmed to beat Garry Kasparov. AlphaGo's algorithms, trained by reinforcement learning, were designed to beat *everyone* using two deep neural networks. One would decide what move to make, and one would judge the probability of winning the overall board.

When they felt ready, in October 2015, the DeepMind team invited the European Go champion, Fan Hui, to their London headquarters. Fan, who'd been playing professionally for almost two decades, was curious. Would they hook electrodes to his brain? Peek inside his head? He was also confident he would win.

But then he didn't.

He lost every game out of the five they played. He was so overwhelmed by emotion afterward that he had to take a walk outside alone.

Fan Hui playing Go at DeepMind's London office. He moved up 300 spots in world rankings after sharpening his game against the machine. (DeepMind Technologies)

Later, he told documentary filmmakers who were shadowing him, "I feel something very strange. I lose with a program, and I don't understand myself anymore."[25]

This captures what it feels like to be a human being bested by a machine at the thing you do best—and, beyond that, better than almost anyone else in the world. Fan's identity, livelihood, and self-image had been linked to his performance at that game.

It was a painful time. His wife told him to stay off the internet because people were trash-talking him, saying he'd been in Europe too long and had lost his competitive edge. It seemed impossible that a computer could beat a human.

Even as good as Fan is at the game, there were better players in the world. Fan's rating was a 2 dan. The world's best ranked player, Lee Sedol, was a 9 dan—the highest rank a grand master can achieve. The next challenge for the team at DeepMind was to pit their computer against Lee, who had 18 world championships under his belt.

Lee was born in South Korea, where Go is such a huge part of the culture that schools there teach strategy. He's one of the best players in the history of the game, famous for creative moves. His passion for it was also a matter of deep pride. He came from a rural background where he was so sheltered, he thought pizza grew on trees.

Still, Lee wasn't afraid to take on a machine, and hordes of reporters were there to document the event.

"I don't want to sound too arrogant," he told a crowd of them amidst the pop of camera flashes. "But still, I think I have the advantage . . . I don't think it will be a very close match."

He was hoping for a shutout. At best, AlphaGo might beat him in one out of their five games.

The team that worked on AlphaGo, meanwhile, was hoping to silence the doubters who thought the Fan Hui match was a fluke.

To ready their software, they'd brought a secret weapon onto their team,

Fan himself. He'd played the machine, probing it for weaknesses, while the machine also kept training itself.

The face-off would involve five matches in March 2016. The team worked feverishly, counting down the days on a whiteboard, tweaking their algorithms until they needed to freeze the code and travel to Seoul, South Korea, where the competition would take place in a hotel, in the presence of dozens of journalists eager to record history as it was made—or not—and the winner would take home a million-dollar prize.

Lee, whose nickname is the Strong Stone, didn't think the software would have improved enough to beat him. "I believe human intuition is still too advanced for AI to have caught up," he told reporters.

But he knew what the stakes were. "I'm doing my best to protect human intelligence," he said.

He wasn't just playing for himself and for his country. This time, he was playing to demonstrate the unique gifts of human beings: the insight and intuition that could never be reduced to lines of code.

The day arrived: a cloudless sky in Seoul, with a smudge of pollution darkening the horizon. Lee strode the hallways with his daughter Lee Hye-rim, passing a gauntlet of reporters. Hye-rim said what many were no doubt thinking: "I'd like it if a machine didn't defeat a human being at Go yet."

Lee sat at the board. He took a long, slow blink. Then he bowed to the human sitting opposite him—the man who'd place the pieces for the machine. After a long, tense pause, Lee placed his first piece. The game was on.

AlphaGo took its time to respond. That pause felt endless and mysterious. Was AlphaGo stuck? Biding its time? Malfunctioning?

And then it moved, a mirror image to Lee's own choice.

As he played, Lee felt as though he was facing more than a machine. "I can feel his mental strength," he said.

In the 60 to 90 seconds between each of AlphaGo's moves, Lee studied the face of the human sitting across from him, perhaps a reflex developed during years of competing with people.

Lee struggled during the game, but as the end drew near, it looked as though AlphaGo had botched things.

"It might be the first mistake . . . that white made," a commentator said.

Another was more definitive. "AlphaGo is making mistakes at the end-game from time to time."

But then the commentator paused for a long moment. At last he explained his silence: "The reason I stopped talking a minute ago was that, according to my count, AlphaGo may have more points."

What had seemed like a mistake wasn't. It had been a calculated move, literally. The math didn't lie, even if the human observers couldn't see the truth of it right away.

The announcer bent over and laughed as if stunned. "I didn't tell you because I couldn't believe it."

Lee Sedol, realizing he's lost to AlphaGo. (DeepMind Technologies)

Lee looked at the board and shook his head, grimacing, as Fan Hui, the only other person who understood the emotional weight of the moment, looked on. "I could feel his pain," Fan said. "He couldn't accept it. It takes time for him to accept the outcome."

Ultimately, AlphaGo won four out of five of the games. Lee won only one, the inverse of his prediction.

The Korean organization that oversees the game awarded AlphaGo an honorary 9 dan rating for the achievement, which in some ways felt reminiscent of the legend of John Henry.

As that story goes, a few years after the end of the Civil War, a Black man named John Henry was a steel driver for the railroad, one of many Black men working this treacherous job for low pay. As a steel driver, Henry hammered a giant drill into solid rock that needed to be moved to make an enormous tunnel.

Henry wasn't a real historical figure, but he symbolized the many Black men who helped build critical infrastructure for a nation that had only recently made it illegal to enslave them.

Wanting to dig the tunnel faster, the railroad company brought in a steam-powered drill that they promised would outstrip the performance of the men on the line. It's not hard to imagine how that felt for the workers to have liberated themselves from bondage only to be made obsolete by machinery.

John Henry was known as the strongest and fastest of all these men. He would be the one to face the machine, to prove that nothing could beat the strength of a skilled Black man.

"If I can't beat this steam drill down," he promised, "I'll die with this hammer in my hand!"

With two 10-pound hammers, he bashed a 14-foot hole in the rock. The machine gave out after 9 feet. John Henry had triumphed. He proved that men beat machines.

But then something horrible happened. John Henry died of exhaustion.

It's a strange tale, creating a hero out of someone who worked himself to death. It's a symbol of the angst that emerged in the Industrial Revolution, when machines were built that could do the work of human beings faster, cheaper, and often better—concentrating wealth in the hands of industry titans while reducing wages for every laborer.

It's also a story we can expect to play out as machine learning wipes out not only jobs that are dangerous, repetitive, and dull, but also the kind that earn high salaries, require years of education, and give people lots of prestige.

It's natural to empathize with people who lose their livelihoods to machinery. Human beings have great capacity for empathy, which is why Lee Sedol imagined his opponent as sentient.

But there is another way to look at the battle of man and machine. Humans made the steam engine. Humans created AlphaGo. They created the 100,000 games' worth of training data. They wrote the algorithms for learning and search that AlphaGo used to win. They sweated and tested and tinkered and tried.

And yes, a champion fell. But it was human beings behind the machine.

So it's possible that a victory for AI is a victory for humanity, after all—or at least for the human beings who own the technology. It all depends on how we use it.

||||||||||||||||||||||||||||||||||

CHAPTER SEVEN

But Can AI Be Clever?

The Deep Blue and AlphaGo victories were extraordinary, but both are still mathematical games. Being human—having a human mind—means we have an incredibly sophisticated understanding of language. We can be witty. Playful. Creative. We can also understand meanings that shift depending on context. For example, the word *dust* can mean particles scattered on a surface or the act of removing that substance.

Deep Blue and AlphaGo showed we could teach computers to think. But could we teach them to think like people?

That was a question that researchers sought to answer with another game using a supercomputer built for that purpose. The game show *Jeopardy!* measures a player's knowledge of trivia and also the ability to figure out the hints buried in the clues. It's a challenge tailor-made for a human mind that is both informed *and* clever. And there's a twist: Contestants have to answer the host's clue with a question. In other words, it's not just knowledge of trivia. Great players have to understand clever wording and syntax.

It takes more than the processing speed to rank a game's next move and its outcomes, as with checkers, chess, or Go. Winning *Jeopardy!* requires an AI to understand context in language well enough to tease an answer out of the data it has learned. That's a tough challenge for a computer.

But Watson was no ordinary supercomputer. It had enough memory and processors to read the equivalent of a million books *per second*, powered by the electrical equivalent of 4,250 human brains.[26] And it was programmed with more than 100 different techniques to understand the clues, come up with possible answers, find and evaluate evidence, and then rank the answers it had generated.[27]

Here's the kind of clue Watson was built to solve:

It was introduced by the Coca-Cola Company in 1963.

The correct answer is, "What is Tab?"

To answer the question, Watson first needed to determine which company first manufactured Tab in 1963. Then it harnessed its natural language capabilities to compute that "introduced by" and "manufactured" meant the same thing in this context. They don't always. For example, your best friend might introduce her dog to you. But it doesn't mean she manufactured the dog unless, say, Rover is a robot.

Even speed and natural language processing weren't enough to win. Watson also had to play strategically. To win *Jeopardy!* you need to know trivia, but you also need to place smart bets. Not all clues are worth the same amount of money, and some, called Daily Doubles, let you bet a specific dollar amount without worrying that the other contestants will buzz in. That's where players can really clean up.

As part of its preparation, the Watson Research team at IBM studied the locations of the three Daily Doubles and found that they were usually in the bottom three rows of clues, especially the fourth row, and also most often in the first column. From there, Watson had to use additional strategies. It had to know how likely it was to get the clue right and how much a bet would help if it was right and cost if it wasn't.

The IBM researchers knew that people are only okay at this sort of thinking. They programmed Watson to gauge the risks versus the rewards using mathematical models that the human brain can't swiftly process.

They did this using a Game State Evaluator, a complex model trained on millions of *Jeopardy!* games between Watson and two simulated human opponents that were modeled after real human ones. The developers used data that told them how accurate humans were when they were fastest to buzz in, how accurate they tended to be on Daily Doubles, and how many Final *Jeopardy!* clues they solved.

That training meant Watson could use its Game State Evaluator and its confidence in the correctness of its answer to figure out the most strategic bet, all in the blink of an eye.

Watson was programmed for every strategic aspect of the game, along with some new insights that the development team discovered on their own. For example, if the leader's score equaled the sum of the two opponents' scores, then Watson learned not to bet to win. Instead, it bet to tie.

Why? Because Watson learned that was better mathematical strategy. If Watson has $20,000 and the two opponents have $13,000 and $7,000, then the safest overall strategy would be betting $6,000. Even with a wrong answer, Watson could tie for first place, if the player with $13,000 places a bad bet and the player with $7,000 gets it right.

In addition to all this strategy, there were practical matters for the IBM team to solve: Watson couldn't see or hear. So they had to figure out how and when to deliver the question to make it fair, along with a robotic thumb for Watson to use to press the buzzer. Watson received the clues via text message at the same time the clue was revealed on the game board. If Watson had a high confidence in its response, it sent a signal to the mechanical thumb mounted on the same kind of buzzer used by human players.

While some people assumed that Watson would always be faster at the buzzer, humans sometimes have an advantage. Human competitors can anticipate when the host is nearly finished reading the clue, and they time their buzz accordingly. Watson couldn't. This meant that on occasion, humans could be faster. But Watson was hard to beat when its confidence was high. Then it could hit the buzzer in just 10 milliseconds.

The best human player ever is Ken Jennings, who won 74 consecutive games and set a Guinness World Record for the most cash ever won on a game show. In 2011, Jennings and another human star, Brad Rutter, faced Watson for three games to see whether human or machine was best.

Jennings went in confident. "I had taken some artificial intelligence classes, and I knew there were no computers that could do what you need to do to win on *Jeopardy!*" he said. "People don't realize how tough it is to write that kind of program that can read a clue in a natural language like English—to understand the puns, the red herrings, to unpack just the meaning of the clue. . . . And I thought, 'Well, this is going to be child's play. Yes, I will come destroy the computer and defend my species.'"[28]

In February 2011, the competition took place—not in *Jeopardy!*'s usual studio in Los Angeles, but at IBM's secret research lab in Yorktown Heights, New York. Watson is too big to move from its climate-controlled home. Instead of a studio audience, onlookers included the IBM brass and their programmers. Millions of dollars of investment were at stake, more than the $1 million prize, but this wasn't for money. It was to see if it could be done; if so, the system could be used for things beyond entertainment.

On the first of three days, competition was stiff. By day's end, Rutter and Watson had each racked up $5,000. Jennings lagged with $2,000. After day two, though, Watson had a huge lead—$35,734 to Rutter's $10,400 and Jennings's $4,800.

But Jennings was a savvy player. No one who'd watched him compete would have counted him out. Luck with the Daily Doubles could bring him back into contention.

Alas, the luck wasn't with him. Watson scored a Daily Double that made it impossible for Jennings, now in second place, to win.

Watson won the grand prize with this clue: "William Wilkinson's *An Account of the Principalities of Wallachia and Moldavia* inspired this author's most famous novel."

The answer: "Who is Bram Stoker?"

Jennings also got it right, but it wasn't enough to stop the bleeding.

On his *Jeopardy!* screen, he wrote, "I, for one, welcome our new computer overlords."[29]

The loss hit Jennings hard. "I felt obsolete. I felt like a Detroit factory worker in the eighties seeing a robot that could now do his job on the assembly line. I felt like 'Quiz Show Contestant' was now the first job that had become obsolete under this new regime of thinking computers."

But he'd do it again "in a heartbeat," he told a *New York Times* reporter: "It's not about the results; this is about being part of the future."

◀ ■ ▶

The leaders at IBM had huge hopes for Watson. Its promise seemed immense: a computer that could answer difficult questions about any subject with speed and accuracy.

IBM called it "the future of knowing"[30] and imagined its software helping out in hospitals, offices, factories, and farms.

But, as happened several times in the history of AI, reality didn't match up with the hopes. IBM engineers underestimated the challenges, even as their aims were noble.

The company started its efforts at unleashing the power of Watson on the world by partnering with medical research centers specializing in cancer. Those centers had lots of data that Watson could use to improve treatments for sick patients.

What seemed like a no-brainer turned out to be hard. The genetic data at IBM's partner was complicated, messy, and incomplete.

So they shifted to another approach: feeding Watson thousands of medical research papers, thinking this might help doctors find additional treatments for their patients. But it didn't turn out to be as useful as they'd hoped, or flexible enough to make it a viable product.

Another project tried to recommend treatments using patients' health records and cancer research, but this was also harder than they thought, in part because Watson couldn't read the doctors' handwritten notes.[31]

So much of the history of AI progress sparks enthusiasm and big promises, followed by setbacks as the full complexity of problems reveals itself—and funding for further study dries up.

But the other part of AI's history is human perseverance. When people keep trying, they solve problems. Even when the solutions take longer than they hope or expect, they find them, powered by the faith of possibility, and sometimes the biggest difference has been made by people who were told they were wasting their time.

PART
II

THE QUEST FOR
THINKING MACHINES

I visualize a time when we will be to robots what dogs
are to humans, and I'm rooting for the machines.[32]
–Claude Shannon

CHAPTER EIGHT

IIIIIIIIIIIIIIIIIIIIIIIIIIIIIIIIII

Brain Vs. Brain

After AlphaGo beat Lee Sedol, the DeepMind team launched a new version called AlphaGo Zero. This version didn't learn from a library of games. At first, the system didn't even know the rules of the game. But by having a goal and time to work toward it, it figured out winning strategies.

And in almost no time, by playing itself, it achieved wonders.

A world champion might rate 3,800 at the game. AlphaGo Zero rates at a 5,000, a rating so good no human is likely ever to beat it. It's come up with strategies people hadn't thought of in thousands of years.

And here's the really fascinating part: The developers aren't sure how it's making decisions.

In this way, it's a lot like the human mind. Our brain is the most complicated organ we have—so complex that we don't fully understand it yet. Scientists aren't completely sure how people think, but in 2018, the journal *Science* published a model for human thought that suggests we think using navigation systems in our brains.[33]

Our brains use two kinds of cells for this: some that tell where we are in space, and some that help us get someplace else. While this system is handy for moving our bodies through the world, it's also used to store mental maps for other things.

Scientists believe your brain makes all sorts of mental maps. They're not just related to geography and navigation. They can apply to situations, objects, and relationships. Your mind uses these maps to make predictions and decisions.

Let's say, for example, you've seen dogs, wolves, and foxes—all members of the Canidae family. You've made a mental map for doglike creatures. This means if you were to see a jackal, your mental mapping system would organize them in with this bunch.

This is true for things besides dogs and their kin. Everything you encounter has physical properties that you automatically use for this kind of categorization. You could organize cars by type and size, food according to fruit, vegetable, bread, and meat. You can even do this with people, and not just with physical attributes but ones like "loves dogs" or "tells bad jokes."[34]

Your brain is great at this sort of activity. This is why you know your favorite band even when you're listening to a song you've never heard before. The sounds conform to patterns you've encountered, even if the track itself is new to you.

Likewise, when you detect a certain scent in the air and maybe even a telltale *pop*, you know somebody's making popcorn. You know a bridge when you see one. When you read, you're recognizing the shapes of the letters and the sounds they correspond to. You're recognizing the words they make. And, guided by their syntax and punctuation and the cues those provide, you understand the meaning of words assembled into sentences.

All of the information that your brain processes is data. Your sense organs take in input—sights, smells, sounds, tastes, textures. This input travels through layers of cells until there is a response.

It's a complex process. Your brain is made of about 100 billion nerve cells, which are called neurons. Each neuron connects with thousands of others using structures called synapses. All day, your neurons send information along these synapses, making millions of new connections every second.

These brain connections make patterns, some of which are stronger than others. When brain cells do this repeatedly, we learn, and the more the pattern is repeated, the stronger the connections get.

These changing connections are us: our memories, our habits, and our personalities—and no two brains are alike.

Here's how a single one of your 100 billion neuron cells fires: a dendrite receives input. The body of the cell processes it, sending it along an axon to a synapse, which is connected to the dendrite of another neuron.

When you multiply this by 100 billion, you begin to grasp the wild activity happening inside your skull.

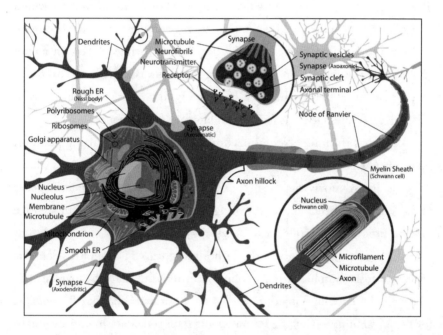

The anatomy of a brain cell. (LadyofHats)

Our brains use these networks of cells to perceive the world, learn, and make decisions. When we encounter familiar data with our sense organs, we recognize it because it matches patterns that we have internalized. This gives us a model for *how* human beings think. But *why* we think is another question.

It turns out that our brains really like certain chemicals. For decades, brain scientists have understood that animals that learn get a burst of a neurotransmitter called dopamine when they receive a reward. Let's say a rat is navigating a maze. At first, it will move at random. When it reaches the end, it gets the snack and the brain chemical that feels good. That provides incentive for the rat to learn the maze. The rat wants to feel those reward chemicals again, so it keeps solving the maze.

This is also how narrow AI functions. Algorithms take data, recognize patterns, and generate outputs that can be used to make assessments and decisions. So in the case of a game like chess, checkers, or Go, algorithms look at the board, consider the moves and their many outcomes, and choose the option most likely to result in an eventual win—the reward. In a reinforcement-learning environment, the more an AI plays, the better it becomes.

Even though algorithms can now beat human beings at certain games and tasks, the human brain remains more powerful. But there are also limits to what biological brains can do. When the amount of data to be processed is vast, artificial intelligence is faster than biological intelligence.

AI also has its limits. Neural networks are great at recognizing patterns. But even when an AI does identify a picture of a bridge, it has no idea what a bridge is. It just knows that the pixels of the photo match the pattern of other photos that are labeled BRIDGE. A bridge means something to a human. We have no proof that a bridge means anything to a computer.

Still, learning to recognize that a bridge appears in a photo is the sort of narrow task computers can accomplish brilliantly. That is, provided they aren't manipulated by something called an *adversarial example*: It's possible for people aiming to trick neural networks to encode data in an image that isn't visible to humans but can make a machine think it's a picture of something else. This has the potential to be dangerous. For example, if someone were to put subtle camouflage stickers on a stop sign meant to fool a self-driving car into thinking it was a yield sign, it could cause horrible wrecks.

In addition to assigning meaning to the patterns we recognize, human brains can also handle a wide range of information, tasks, and physical challenges. Computers currently excel when the task is narrow. Machines aren't yet as powerful or as complex as human brains, and anything that requires robotics and AI is enormously complex.

Even though computer processing speed can beat a human brain at a lot of narrow tasks, in other areas, they can't compete. Although there are large AI models that have hundreds of billions of neurons—and in some cases more—biological brain neurons do more complicated things than artificial ones. For now, your human mind wins.

But this won't always be the case.

◄ ■ ►

Moravec's paradox and what we keep getting wrong

As amazing as the human brain is, AI keeps surprising us with its power.

Before Deep Blue beat Garry Kasparov, for example, chess was viewed as the ultimate test of intelligence. No machine could possibly have the insight and creativity of a grand master, right?

Wrong.

Likewise, no machine could beat a human at Go.

Or at *Jeopardy!*—that's what the human champions believed.

They all learned the same lesson: that human intelligence isn't as special as they thought.

So how do you avoid being an overconfident human?

It helps to understand some of the differences between biological and artificial brains. Even though neural networks are based on how we think the human brain operates, there are differences between the capabilities of artificial brains and biological ones.

A computer can multiply two 20-digit numbers with speed and accuracy. This would be hard for even a math champ.

But a human can button a shirt, tie shoes, or fix a bowl of cereal with milk—things that would be tough to accomplish for an AI-powered robot.

Human beings *think* the multiplication challenge is hard. We *think* getting dressed and eating breakfast is easy. But when it comes to the computational power each task takes, we have it backward.

That makes it a paradox. What's a paradox? Something that defies common sense but is still true.

For example, sometimes you can save money by spending money. How is this possible? Well, if you spend $50 to fix your brakes before they get too worn, you can save hundreds of dollars in repairs later. Or if you buy a product you use all the time on sale even if you haven't run out, you will eventually come out ahead financially.

There's a paradox in AI, at least when it comes to robotics.

For a human brain, reasoning takes a whole lot of computational energy. But sensory and motor-perception skills don't. The reverse is true for computers. This is called Moravec's paradox. It defies logic. Even so, this paradox is why a server in a diner is less likely to lose their job to AI than a financial analyst. We're used to classifying jobs as "low skilled" and "high skilled" and being snobby about which one is more difficult. The AI revolution will upend all of this, and it's what makes this technological shift different from past ones.

In the past, technology tended to replace workers who were considered "low skilled" because their work didn't require a lot of computation. That won't always be the case going forward. A lot of people who have spent a long time refining their computational skills are going to end up feeling stunned and blindsided in the same way the former world champions of chess, Go, and *Jeopardy!* did when they lost to machines.

There's a persistent tendency to overestimate the specialness of human intelligence. At the same time, there's a tendency to underestimate the incredible physical things we're able to do and how hard that is to replicate in a machine.

It takes a lot of human brain power to be good at games like Go, chess, and *Jeopardy!* But it takes less for computers—and our ability to build faster and more powerful machines keeps increasing.

And it's not just games that AI is good at. It's all forms of discovering patterns in data and making predictions, recommendations, and decisions. It's likely to continue taking us by surprise when we discover fascinating things neural networks can do.

Part of this comes from our bias that human intelligence is a universal form of intelligence. We first assumed that humans were the only intelligent animal.

But then an animal behaviorist named B. F. Skinner trained pigeons to bowl, play Ping-Pong, and read signs that read TURN and PECK.[35] He also taught his cats to play piano and the family dog to play hide-and-seek. His animals learned these tasks by being conditioned with rewards—the same idea behind the reinforcement learning used to train AI.

To teach a pigeon to turn when the letters *t-u-r-n* appeared on a small screen, for example, he rewarded the pigeon every time it started to turn. Eventually, with enough rewards given for movements, the pigeon associated the letters with that turning motion.[36] It learned *p-e-c-k* the same way.

With experiments like this, we've had to let go of the idea that humans are the only animal with intelligence. Humans do have a greater capacity to learn than pigeons. But animals can think and learn to do extraordinary things, from rats being outfitted with tiny backpacks and sent to rescue earthquake survivors to pigs being trained to play video games with their snouts.

Another thing we tend to do is assume that human intelligence is the highest sort that can be achieved. When you think about it,

B. F. Skinner used reinforcement learning to teach pigeons to turn, read, and play Ping Pong. (From "'Self-Awareness' in the Pigeon." Reprinted with permission from AAAS.)

it's funny: a group of beings pondering what intelligence is and deciding that they're the measure of it. We don't have an unbiased perspective, nor do we really know how we make our decisions.

Those world champion chess, Go, and *Jeopardy!* players were wrong about what it took to succeed at their games. What felt like creativity to them was actually something that could be broken down and solved mathematically—and better done by machines than by even the most talented people.

AlphaGo Zero, which competed against itself and updated its own system as it learned, devised a system with breakthrough thinking capacity. Simply put, it thought in ways humans don't.

As it played Go, it discovered strategies that humans have used and refined for a millennium. Eventually, though, it stopped playing the way people do and followed its own strategy. No one had ever seen Go played this way before. In short, AlphaGo Zero developed and displayed a new type of problem-solving—a new type of intelligence.

This technology isn't limited to use in games. Deep neural networks can be used to study all sorts of human problems, from diseases such as cancer to climate change and poverty. The results AI generates could offer insights human beings might not have considered. This is part of the enormous promise of artificial intelligence. It's going to think of things that we don't.

The faster and more powerful computers get, the more of this will be possible. Computers will someday have more power than the human brain. Human brains have to fit inside of our skulls, which means brains can get only so big. They have 100 billion connections and are wildly powerful. But eventually we will figure out how to make machines capable of making more neural connections—this could happen as soon as 2050, according to some researchers,[37] while others believe the timeline ranges from further out to never.

The point in time when machines overtake humans is known as "the singularity." If it comes about, it will occur when we create an artificial intelligence so powerful it invents tools beyond anything our human minds could produce. To imagine how this might feel, think about your average dog. It might be smart, but you're smarter. Now imagine that you're the dog in the scenario, watching as the superior mind invents an even better one, and so on and so forth. In the same way no human player will ever beat AlphaGo, no human mind will be able to keep up once the singularity has occurred.

What will that mean for humanity if we bring about the singularity?

No one really knows.

◀ ■ ▶

AI and human intelligence have many similarities, but the differences are just as important. Understanding this is vital if we want AI to be safe and helpful—instead of harmful—for humanity.

Ideally, the world will have room for both AI and human intelligence.

Human vs. Artificial Intelligence

Human Intelligence	Artificial Intelligence
Human intelligence is analog. Everything we know is encoded in our bodies. When we know something, it's in our heads and ours alone.	**Artificial intelligence is faster.** The speed of human thought is about 120 meters per second. AI systems can process at nearly the speed of light, which is 29,927,458 meters per second. This allows algorithms to solve complex math problems faster, letting an AI quickly identify two matching photos in a collection of a billion photos. That would take a human being ages.
Human intelligence is siloed. We can write, speak, and communicate with gestures. But we can't, say, bump knuckles and transfer knowledge to each other directly.	**Artificial intelligence is portable.** You can take software and data from one computer and move it to another. But you can't do this with people.
Humans learn with less data. We learn and generalize with a small amount of data. After you've seen a cat or two, you know one.	**Artificial intelligence needs a lot of data.** It might need to see a million cats to recognize the underlying patterns.
Human learning is hard to update. Is Pluto a planet, or isn't it? As information changes, we have to keep on top of it. Meanwhile, we tend to forget things.	**AI is easy to update.** Algorithms can be tweaked. Systems can be upgraded.

◀ ■ ▶

Early robots: pants optional

Around 1495, Leonardo da Vinci sketched plans for a robotic knight that could sit, stand, move its arms and legs, and open the visor on its armor. Leonardo had no idea that a fully autonomous robotic soldier would be harder to build than an AI that could make his *Mona Lisa* painting speak.

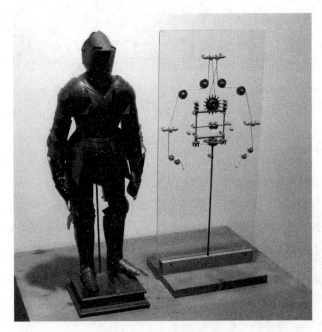

Leonardo da Vinci's mechanical knight, built from his notebooks. (Erik Möller)

In the 18th century, a Swiss watchmaker named Pierre Jaquet-Droz built intricate devices with thousands of parts. One automaton could dip a goose-feather quill into a pot of ink, shake it off, and write as its eyes tracked its progress. Another could draw several pictures and even blow dust from its artwork using a hidden bellows. A third played songs on a flute using its 10 movable fingers.

These clockwork creations by Pierre Jaquet-Droz contained thousands of parts. (Rama)

In 1868, the *Saturday Evening Post* called an automaton named Mr. Steam Man an "eighth wonder of the world." Created by Zadoc Dederick, Mr. Steam Man was seven foot nine, weighed 500 pounds, and wore a stovepipe hat and gloves (but no pants). Using its coal-powered steam-engine torso, it could walk 30 miles per hour.

These inventions assumed that intelligence could be built into human-like constructions. Each tackled the motor-perception challenges. But now we know that those functions are actually harder for true AI-powered robots than purely cognitive tasks are for neural networks.

Mr. Steam Man chugs along without pants.

CHAPTER NINE

IIIIIIIIIIIIIIIIIIIIIIIIIIIIIII

AI Is like a Sandwich

If a single-neuron Perceptron is like a bread-and-butter sandwich, a deep neural network is like a fancy sandwich with a lot of ingredients in the middle. Those ingredients are the additional neurons.

The input layer and output layer are the slices of bread.

In between are the hidden layers, potentially a lot of them. As with sandwiches, the middle is where the magic happens—and it's pure math.

Neural networks understand the world using math. This means they need to be given data that has been expressed in numbers. There are tons of ways to do this, and one challenge for engineers is to figure out the quantifiable features that matter most.

So how do you describe something in math? In a black-and-white image, the brightness of each pixel is a number. In a color image, each pixel is made of a percentage of red, blue, and green—also a number.

Think about sound waves. What is the height of the wave? What is its frequency? Those qualities can be expressed as numbers.

How many words are in this sentence? Seven.

What about the letters? You can assign numbers to represent them. A = 00000, B = 00111, C = 11100, D = 11011 and so on.

As Claude Shannon demonstrated, communication isn't random. If you type the letters *t* and *h*, a vowel will usually come next. This is how autocomplete tries to help you finish words you've started to type. It can also try to predict the next word. This is because letters and words have underlying mathematical relationships with each other.

Some letters and some words tend to appear more closely together, which boosts their probability of being the next to be used. The distance between them can be measured with vectors—a mathematical concept. All of this counts as the sort of data that can be used by algorithms in a neural network.

This is a big deal. Some physicists believe you can represent *everything* with math: The world and beyond—the entire universe, with you and me in it—is potentially built of particles whose properties can be described mathematically.

Max Tegmark, a physics professor at MIT, is so certain of this that he says, "If my idea is wrong, physics is ultimately doomed. But if the universe really is mathematics, there's nothing we can't, in principle, understand."[38]

So that's the potential of artificial intelligence, at least according to Tegmark: It can help us understand the universe. (And that would take an impossibly large computer, but Tegmark's enthusiasm is understandable, if extreme.)

Let's go back to the bread of our analogy.

The input layer is where you feed your neural network numerical data. There can be many input neurons. Each one captures a characteristic of the data expressed as a number.

Let's say you're trying to train a network to recognize handwriting.

Your input layer provides the neural network with data on each pixel in the handwriting sample.

Each feature in your input layer is assigned a value between 0 and 1. Each input neuron sends its number to every neuron in the next layer.

And now to the middle of the sandwich.

The first hidden layer processes data on clusters of pixels: say, the small lines and curved shapes that are part of each letter. The layer takes those numbers and combines them. The goal is to see if the input layer matches the data the network received during training. How close is the image to the expected lines and curves that are part of the important features of handwriting?

◄ ■ ►

These are not yes or no questions like a Perceptron can handle. Instead, they're mathematical questions. Each neuron in the first hidden layer calculates how much emphasis the data should receive. Then the number is squished to be somewhere between 0 and 1. The result gets sent to every neuron in the next layer.

The next layer in a handwriting analysis module examines clusters of clusters. Those would be whole circles and strokes made of the previous layer's clusters. Then the result goes to the next layer, and so on.

Hidden layers are called that because the math that's happening in them can't be observed directly—only its effects.

The more hidden layers there are, the more complex the math gets. As developers fine-tune the weights, those adjustments affect all the other neurons in the layers beyond that one. It's like a multidimensional spiderweb. Tug one strand and all the others will move.

The final layer—the other slice of bread in the sandwich—is the output.

The output layer assembles those shapes to figure out the probability it is that the input letter was an *A* or a *T*.

There can be one output, or many. If you're only wanting to find the letter *A*, then there is one output. But if you're identifying all the letters and numbers a person might write, then there will be many.

However many output neurons you have, each one shows the probability that the image matches the label.

After you design the architecture of your neural network, which is kind of like a recipe, you have to adjust the math to improve its performance. To continue with the recipe analogy, this is like adjusting the amounts of your ingredients.

But it's complicated. A lot can go awry with your inputs and with the hidden layers. This is where the sandwich analogy falls short. In a sandwich, the pickle doesn't alter the cheese. But the weights of neurons in one layer change the math, and this change ripples to the other layers.

This means developers do lots of testing and adjustments to get acceptable results.

We do this all the time as people: make observations and find patterns and use the data we've taken in with our senses to predict what we'll hear and see next. It's harder for computers. Developers help with constructing algorithms that can let a machine learn all on its own along the way—just as your brain works.

Let's say you're trying to get an AI to categorize apples, oranges, and lemons.

You'd choose a few properties: shape, weight, color, skin texture, basing your choices on observations that can be measured. Each fruit is going to have a range of measurements for the features you choose, and there will be clusters of data that have averages for each fruit.

Your human brain could graph this data if you had just one or two properties. But as soon as you get more than will fit on an X, Y, and Z axis, then the neural network is going to be able to calculate results much better than you—this is why in certain tasks, such as reading X-rays, artificial intelligence can sometimes outperform human beings.

When it works, results are astounding.

But they're also black boxes, at least at this point. We knew how Deep Blue made all of its decisions. But the same is not true for deep convolutional neural networks.

We know what goes in and what comes out. We don't yet know exactly what's happening in those hidden layers, where the network learns on its own. We can see what happens when we adjust the weights in each layer and whether those adjustments get better or worse results—but the rest of the middle? That's a mystery, same as the human brain.

◀ ■ ▶

Diving down:
Training deep neural networks

Back propagation is short for "back propagation of errors," which is a process for correcting errors. It's called that because it adjusts weights of all the neurons in a network that contribute to an error.

This is one of the things engineers do when they're training neural networks. They look at what the algorithms generate based on the training data. They compare this to what they expected. They're trying to make the difference between what they expected and what the algorithm generated as small as possible. Neurons that aren't weighted properly cause this difference, and some mis-weighted neurons are more responsible for it than others.

Finding the best weights for a neural network's architecture is called optimization, and this is an important step in the process. But it's not the end.

The next phase is to show the AI data that it hasn't already seen. Can it answer new questions? If so, then it is working.

But coders might need to do more back propagation on the new data to make sure the neural network's output matches the training data. This is called *fitting to the training data*.

Sometimes neural networks can get *too* good at this.

Computers are great at seeing patterns, but some of the patterns they see are coincidental. If they take these meaningless coincidences they learned from training and apply them to new data, they won't get good results. When that happens, it's called overfitting.

One example of this: Between 2000 and 2009, Americans ate more mozzarella cheese and also earned more doctorates in engineering. The graphs of these two things might look alike, but they don't actually have anything to do with each other.[39]

One way to avoid overfitting is to use different data for testing the AI than you used for training it. That's called a train/test split. The goal isn't to match the training data exactly. It's to get the most accurate output possible when you introduce new data the network hasn't seen (and you have to hope that data matches the real world).

◀ ■ ▶

So where does all this data for training a neural network come from? Very often, you generate it. Every time you post a photo, click a link, or interact with social media—say, by following a hashtag—you generate data. You can also generate it by being out in the world, which increasingly has cameras filming you, radio-frequency identification technology, and the less exotic checkout stands where you're using credit and debit cards. (There's also such a thing as synthetic data; we'll get to that later.)

Data doesn't come from only people, and it's not about only people. A virus has features that can be measured, for example, and those measurements can provide all sorts of data. Some of the first neural networks (collections of algorithms) were trained with large collections of images.

Wherever the data comes from, it's what's used to train AI—and algorithms learn a lot like people do. When it's created, AI doesn't know anything. It's like a baby. When you were a baby, your brain had a lot of rapid learning to do, and you did this using your senses. The data you absorbed is what taught you about the world and how it works. AI at this point is nowhere near as sophisticated as a human brain, but it does learn by using data. The people training AI give it the data.

There are two ways to train a neural network. Let's start with something called *supervised learning*. If someone showed you a picture of a blobfish and said, "This is a blobfish," you'd learn the common name for this really strange-looking pink fish. The more of these pictures you saw, the better you'd get at recognizing a blobfish. Eventually, you might even recognize one if you saw just a tiny bit of it, or a blobfish from an unexpected angle.

This is called supervised learning because someone who knew the answer told you what you were looking at. AI can learn in the same way. The first step is to feed the AI a set of data: blobfish pictures that are labeled BLOB-FISH. The next step is to feed the AI more data and let the AI decide whether something is a blobfish or not.

This yes/no answer structure is important. AI is good at yes/no questions, and one of the challenges for developers is to structure data so that it can be viewed through this binary lens.

When the AI has evaluated all the pictures with a "yes, blobfish," or "no, not blobfish" answer, the training supervisor checks the answers. The supervisor lets the AI know when it got something wrong. AI learns from its mistakes. If it can correctly categorize an image that it hasn't seen before, then it's learning.

With *unsupervised learning*, AI is given data *without* labels, and by recognizing the underlying patterns, it learns what objects are. Engineers at Google, for example, set up an unsupervised learning network with 16,000 computer processors and fed them 10 million YouTube videos selected at random. The network recognized patterns, not particularly accurately at first. But it eventually learned to recognize whether something was a cat or a person.

You already intuitively understand how this works. Let's say you saw a number of round, flat objects at the beach. Some were whole. Some, broken. You knew from observing their shapes, colors, and sizes that they were all the same thing. And then when someone told you, "That's a sand dollar," you would be able to both identify and label it afterward. Even before you knew its name, you had absorbed enough data about sand dollars to know what a new or even partial sand dollar was the next time you encountered one.

There's also *reinforcement learning*, which is AI that learns by trial and error. Something called a reward function tells the network whether its output is right or wrong. Like a rat in a maze getting rewarded with cheese or a person beating a level in a video game, the reward helps train the AI. It's engineered to maximize the rewards it receives. It also wants to minimize the penalties, and it figures out the best strategy for that on its own.

All three types of training can be used in *deep learning*, which is the most like human learning. With deep learning, a computer model learns from existing knowledge and applies it to a new set of data. Deep learning is present in any neural network with more than one hidden layer. This technique has helped driverless cars recognize things like stop signs and tell the difference between a pedestrian and a mailbox. It's also what powers voice control on your phone and other devices—for a long time that was considered a hard problem, but now the solution is everywhere.

Key Terms to Know

What's an algorithm?

Algorithms are the instructions a computer uses to solve a problem.

What's a neural network?

When you put together a bunch of algorithms trained to recognize patterns and interpret data, you have a neural network. Neural networks have three kinds of layers: input, hidden, and output.

Input layers are where you feed the network data. For example, a database of photos, some of which contain pictures of cats.

Hidden layers are between the input and the output. Hidden layers take the input, and multiply it by weights. The weight of a layer controls the strength of the signal between neurons. Weights can be raised or lowered to make it harder or easier for the neurons to fire. Inputs are multiplied by their weights and added together. Then a number called a bias is added. This helps developers adjust the neuron activation function to better fit the data. That helps get more accurate output values.

Output layers give the results of the data you're interpreting. In a one-layer neural network: YES, this is a cat or NO, this is not a cat. Or, with a deep neural network, you get a percentage probability that something is a cat, rather than a yes-or-no answer.

CHAPTER TEN

IIIIIIIIIIIIIIIIIIIIIIIIIIIIII

The Trouble with Pure Logic

In the movie *Fantasia*, Mickey Mouse plays a sorcerer's apprentice. But it's not all cauldrons and wands for poor Mickey—it's more like boring buckets and mops. That's why Mickey decides to borrow the sorcerer's magic hat one day when his boss goes out.

Mickey enchants a broom, and while it's hauling water for him, he naps. There's just one problem. The broom doesn't know to stop, and by the time Mickey wakes up, the room is full of water. Mickey can't figure out how to end his spell, so he chops up the broom. Then each splinter becomes a new broom, carrying more water. It's a disaster that only the magician can solve.

This sometimes happens to developers who are trying to get AI to perform certain tasks. So much can go wrong. It seems obvious, but one reason for it is that AI isn't the same as human intelligence.

Human intelligence has an emotional component. We can often figure out what someone means by assessing their beliefs or their mental or emotional state. This capacity is part of something called *theory of mind*. When used in a psychological context, it describes the ability to perceive that another being has a mind. Theory of mind lets us intuit the mindset of others, and sometimes interpret and predict their behavior, without even being aware that we're doing this.

This is why when someone says, "Nothing is wrong, I'm *fine*," you might understand that they are actually not fine. It's also why if someone tells you,

"Go get me that bag on the counter," you intuit that they mean the bag and its contents, not just the bag.

That's theory of mind at work.

An AI-powered robot would not be able to do the same thing. It would be more likely to dump out the contents and bring you the bag alone. AI can't read your emotional states and make inferences, at least not yet—but people are working on that. AI also isn't good at cultural context.

For now, it's good to think of AI as a sorcerer's hat. It's going to do what you ask, with sometimes surprising and terrible results.

How do you avoid Mickey's fate?

Understanding what machine learning is good at is an essential place to start. It's called narrow artificial intelligence for a reason. Machine learning today works for narrow tasks.

Find the best pancake recipe is a narrow task.

Find the best pancake recipe and then cook the pancake is not. (Both of these things have been done by AI, by the way—just not by the same one.)

Trying to solve too broad a problem with AI won't work. But it's not the only mistake. Here are some other potential pitfalls:

- You didn't provide enough data.
- The data is biased, confusing, or irrelevant.
- You trained it improperly—either on a task that was unrealistic or too simple.
- You asked it to do something you didn't mean for it to do.

While it might seem like artificial intelligence failures—the Mickey moments—are failures of technology, they're not. The errors AI makes are all human errors.

Artificial intelligence isn't like human intelligence—it doesn't have the context to understand what we're really asking when we ask for something, and if we aren't careful at every step, we'll get results that are unhelpful or worse.

Let's say, for example, you code a reinforcement-learning agent to play Tetris, a game that challenges users to fit blocks together in solid horizontal lines. When users do this, the blocks disappear. When players fail and the blocks reach the top of the screen, they lose.

One developer trying to teach an AI to play Tetris ran into a problem when his bot figured out that it could avoid losing by pausing the game. This shortcut met the definition of success: It didn't lose!

But it wasn't the intention of the developer, either—the developer wanted the agent to develop strategies for playing Tetris well enough to keep the game going, not skirt loss by pressing the PAUSE button.

This kind of shortcut is known as "reward hacking." It's getting a reward without doing the work, and it's a common problem. It doesn't crop up only with games.

One developer tried to train a robotic arm to make pancakes and toss them onto a plate. She gave her robot arm rewards every time it avoided dropping a pancake on the floor, thinking that would keep the pancake in the pan or on the plate. Instead, the robot concluded that throwing the pancake as far as possible would also work. Without meaning to, the programmer invented a pancake launcher.

Another developer was trying to teach a robot not to run into walls. This is the sort of thing that would be useful for a delivery robot in a hospital, where crashing into the walls could be a particular problem. Imagine if it was carrying pills or samples of blood, feces, or urine. Yikes!

As the developer trained the robot, it came up with a surefire way of avoiding walls. It evolved not to move. Not moving is a good way to not crash into walls, it turns out. But it's not useful, either.

Next, the developer required the robot to move. The robot found another way to hack rewards. It moved—but in circles. Again, the robot didn't hit the walls, but it's not what the developer meant.

Part of the challenge in coding is to anticipate the many creative solutions an algorithm will find for a problem, and then make sure an appropriate solution is the one that gets the rewards.

Sometimes we train neural networks to look for the wrong thing entirely by accident. A neural network programmed to recognize sheep was great at recognizing sheep in grassy fields, but not so great at identifying them in unexpected places. This meant the network had learned to recognize grass, not sheep.

That's kind of a funny error. But the same failure can be catastrophic if it's not discovered. For example, a group of researchers was trying to use machine learning to identify cancer cells from photographs of samples. They accidentally trained their neural network to recognize the presence of rulers in photos.

How did this happen? Photographs of cancerous growths often have a ruler next to the tumor to show its size. It's something people training the neural networks didn't notice. But the AI did, and so it took a shortcut. It didn't understand rulers or cancer—just the frequency with which they appeared together in training data, which was enough to give it results that looked accurate but weren't. That error was caught. It's conceivable, though, that other errors like this might not be discovered. Obviously, diagnosing cancer is high stakes, which is why having clean data is paramount.

Glitches like these are called *alignment problems*, meaning unintended results that happen when the systems we teach do something other than what we wanted them to do. Many alignment problems get caught in the development phase: first, when programmers are making sure the goal is well defined; later, as they're scrubbing errors and extraneous material from data; and finally, when ensuring the AI actually generated a solution that solves the problem it was meant to solve.

The more automated systems there are out there in the world, the more likely alignment problems are to happen. And there are a lot of AI systems at work already, with more to come. There are important questions to ask: What problems are being investigated by AI in the first place? Who benefits from the work, and who pays for its mistakes? For example, if humans write algorithms and create neural networks meant to predict crime, who is harmed by biased algorithms? Who detects the harm? Who was meant to be kept safe in the first place?

This is why it's so important to take care at every step of the way. Artificial minds see patterns and make predictions and recommendations based on them. If biased or contaminated data leads to poor predictions and recommendations, it's not the fault of the neural network. Human beings are the ones who provide the training data and set the goals, and who either benefit or suffer because of the technology. If people suffer from discrimination because of software, human beings, and not code, are to blame.

◀ ■ ▶

How would you use artificial intelligence to generate the ideal recipe for fluffy pancakes? A British software company that usually works with automakers on car engines and prototypes took a detour to do just that to entertain themselves during the COVID-19 lockdown.[40]

First, they looked at 800 recipes. From those, they chose 31 recipes that had enough user reviews to train their model. The user reviews helped make the predictions for what pancakes would be fluffiest. Then the developers cleaned their data to make sure there weren't human errors that would generate bad results.

A machine learning algorithm made hundreds of thousands of calculations to determine the right ingredients.

In studying the seven essential ingredients of pancakes, they learned there were five key ingredients to fluffy pancakes: flour, baking powder, sugar, milk, and butter. (The eggs and salt don't play into fluffiness as much.)

Baking powder makes CO_2 form, a gas that makes batter bubble. The flour has gluten molecules, and the sugar, milk, and butter, which contain fat, develop the gluten.

When those molecules combine, they form a web of proteins that trap the air and make bubbles. And that's what makes good pancakes fluffy.

Finally, sugar helps with something called the Maillard reaction. That's what makes food turn golden brown.

They didn't train the AI on cooking techniques, just the ingredients. But pancakes are pretty standard, as is described below.

Here's how to make Perfect AI Pancakes:

Ingredients

210 grams of flour

48 grams of sugar

14 grams of baking powder

6 grams of salt

2 eggs

256 grams of milk

25 grams of butter, melted

Procedure

Combine the dry ingredients in one bowl and the wet ingredients in another bowl.

Then mix them both together. Don't overmix—that gives you chewy pancakes.

Heat a griddle or frying pan over medium heat on an electric stove or low on a gas stove. Lightly grease the pan.

Pour some pancake mix to the pan or use a ladle to create the size pancakes you want. Be sure not to crowd the pan; you'll probably be able to fit between two and four pancakes in a frying pan.

Cook until open bubbles form on top.

Gently flip the pancake and cook for another half a minute or so, until browned.

||||||||||||||||||||||||||||||||||

CHAPTER ELEVEN

Can AI Read Your Mind?

"You're so emotional!" is never a compliment. This bias against the human capacity to feel is nothing new.

Plato described emotion and reason as two horses pulling in opposite directions. Centuries later, the philosopher René Descartes wrote, "I think, therefore I am." He meant our senses can't be trusted as proof of our existence. Only the rational mind, which is capable of doubting, is proof that that we are actually here.

There's bias against emotion in the sciences, too. Emotions are seen as fuzzy and hard to quantify and certainly less important to human survival than reason. Given the human love affair with rational processes, it would be understandable to assume that we'd be better off if we could ditch our emotions.

That would be a huge mistake.

It is true, of course, that emotions can sometimes get in the way. If your body is flooded with emotion, your mind sometimes has a hard time focusing. This is what happened to Garry Kasparov when he was playing chess against Deep Blue. He blamed his loss on losing his fighting spirit.

But there's a flip side. When we can't feel our emotions, we can't think effectively. Emotions help us make decisions.

A doctor named Antonio Damasio cared for patients who had disorders with their frontal lobes. That's the part of the brain that communicates with the limbic system, which houses our emotions and helps us make memories.

His patients had normal intelligence. They did fine on tests. But not all was normal with their lives. People with these injuries couldn't access their emotions. And it turns out this is a major disability.

You might think that people freed from emotion would make better decisions. But this is not the case. A mind unchecked by emotion will dutifully generate option after option and run through all of the scenarios without landing on a decision.

Without access to emotion, it's hard to distinguish among the available options. For example, most of us would get embarrassed if we couldn't decide what to wear and we were late to work. Not so for people who can't feel.

People with this disability also make bad decisions because they're missing the normal feedback that follows poor choices. If you make a bad decision—say, you tell a lie and get busted—you will probably feel awful afterward. That feeling teaches you not to make the same bad decision again. Without your emotions helping you form patterns of behavior to repeat and behavior to avoid, it's more difficult to act rationally. Your heart and your mind are both necessary.

We also rely on our ability to perceive and understand each other's emotions to communicate. If you went up to a friend in tears and they laughed at you or didn't respond at all, you'd probably be upset. It might end the friendship. Relationships depend on emotional connection, not just rational exchanges.

Because the purpose of machine learning is to make predictions and decisions, it stands to reason that artificial intelligence would work better as a tool meant to assist human beings when it's equipped with emotional intelligence.

This might sound strange at first. Computers can't possibly feel, not before artificial general intelligence, right? Also, it might be also easy to assume that the lack of emotions in machines is a *good* thing—decisions based on pure data are better than ones based on messy human emotion, right?

That's probably not the case. Many experts in machine learning believe that a capacity to recognize and even express emotion is probably as necessary for machines as it is for human beings. A field called affective computing, founded by the MIT professor Rosalind Picard, has organized itself around this idea.

We spend a lot of time interacting with our computers, sometimes even more than we interact with other people. Picard noted this in 1998, well before the

Rosalind Picard (David Bruce, cropped by Disavian)

invention of deep neural networks, and before social media platforms like Meta, TikTok, and Snapchat, which hook people into spending even more time online.

If the devices we use for so much time lack the capacity to recognize our emotional states when we're using them, then we can expect AI systems to fail in the same way that human beings fail when they can't feel.

"Computers, if they are to be truly effective at decision making, will have to have emotions or emotion-like mechanisms," Picard wrote in a groundbreaking book called *Affective Computing*.

Communication is complicated. We often think that words are the best communication tools that we have. After all, human beings have developed thousands of languages with millions of words. These languages use different alphabets. Some use characters instead of alphabets. Each language has a particular system of grammar. Altogether, these are tools that help us understand and be understood.

For all of this complexity, our bodies are equally vital communication tools. Humans are generally good at reading nonverbal cues: eye contact, facial expressions, postures, gestures, and tone of voice. There's a whole lot of data that we convey along with our words when we're talking face-to-face, and even over something like Zoom.

Without nonverbal communication aids, we can't convey all of what we intend to. Very often, words alone don't do the trick. This is why emoticons and emoji are so popular. It might not surprise you to know that the smile emoticon came first, invented in 1982 by a professor at Carnegie Mellon University. Even professors communicating in the relatively early days of email didn't want their colleagues and students to think they were mad.

Our emotional states contribute to our ability to connect with and understand each other. Body language is also a useful system for getting vital feedback. We generally look to the reactions of others to modulate our behavior and what we say when we're communicating in good faith, because we want to understand and to be understood.

The same could be true for machine learning. In theory, the better our machines can read us, the better we can communicate. This will help us get what we want and need. Once again, data will be key. And here, all of our nonverbal communication—from our facial expressions to gestures, tone of voice, and even heart rate—can be turned into data that machines can use to make predictions and decisions based on our emotional states.

This essentially gives computers a simulated theory of mind, at least when it comes to understanding the mental state of a user.

When computers don't understand what we want, it can sometimes be frustrating. Let's say you've just moved to Paris, Texas. Your location is not turned on because you have privacy concerns. You want pizza, so you search for "best pizza in Paris," and the only results that come up are for ones in Paris, France, which is almost 5,000 miles away. You might get hangry. You might want to smash your device.

A device that could recognize your emotional state would recognize your frustration and would know the initial results had been a bust. It would then prompt you to turn on your location settings or to specify which Paris you meant.

Machines don't need to have organic feelings of their own to recognize this. They can be programmed to recognize the data that our feelings generate to adjust course.

This is the big idea behind affective computing—to create machine awareness of a user's state of mind. In its ideal form, it builds trust between us and the machines we interact with, and it also makes people better at what we're trying to do.

Take driving, for example. There's a car crash every 5 seconds. Someone dies in a car wreck every 13 minutes, and car crashes are the leading cause of death for people under 35. Many car crashes are caused by human error.

The stakes are high every time a driver gets behind the wheel. So how can affective computing ensure that people don't mess up?

By assessing the emotional state of the driver. There are systems that use cameras and microphones to capture the facial expressions and speech of drivers. They can also measure breathing and heart rate, how tightly a driver is gripping a wheel, even palm sweat—all potential signs of stress. AI analyzes this data and uses it to see if a driver is distracted, tired, agitated, or otherwise at risk.

A company called Affectiva, which started at MIT, has trained deep neural network using more than 8 million faces. When it detects dangerous levels of stress, it can reduce the temperature inside the car, suggest relaxing music, and even change the voice of the GPS to create an empathetic bond with the driver.[41]

There's also potential for the use of human-made algorithms meant to detect emotions in classrooms. When students are anxious, they have a harder time retaining information, following lessons, and even answering questions.[42] Classroom devices that recognize when kids need comfort, a deep breath, food, rest, or other intervention could help students do better in school—provided the system is used to support students and not punish them. While it seems obvious to many that schools should provide emotional support, it's also true that in the US, 19 states permit the paddling of students in schools—a clear sign that punishment is perceived as an educational tool in those places.

In addition to risks, there are limits. An app can recognize a smile or a sign of distress. It can measure the facial expressions in a movie theater full of people and get a good sense of whether they like what they're watching.[43] A wearable device can detect that you're producing a lot of cortisol, a stress hormone. It can suggest you take a break. Or if you're getting frustrated in a voicemail maze, the chatbot can measure your vocal tones and route you to a human helper sooner.

If an algorithm knows your emotional state, there is a risk it can use that information to manipulate you. What's more, facial expressions aren't necessarily a clear window into your emotions. People can smile for all sorts of reasons, and it doesn't always mean they're happy. A smile can mask anger or fear. Different cultures smile for different reasons. Some people have good poker faces. Some people are skilled liars.

Software also can't look at a face and guess your intentions based on your expression. Let's say an airport has a device to screen the faces of people passing. There's no technology that can say, "That person intends to hijack a plane."

This is where certain uses of affective computing algorithms are problematic. The US Department of Homeland Security is using them to predict potential threats. Other nations with different privacy norms are using mass surveillance to monitor communications data. Some companies are using it to screen applications for jobs and loans.

A video job interview can't determine whether the candidate will be competent based on their facial expressions or voice. There are companies that make this promise, though. We can expect to see more instances of AI that makes false promises.

This is where we ought to be careful, scientists say.

Jonathan Gratch of the University of Southern California's Institute for Creative Technologies put it like this: "When companies and governments claim these capabilities, the buyer should beware because often these techniques have simplistic assumptions built into them that have not been tested scientifically."[44]

But that's software built with arguably good intentions. What is the intention behind measuring a person's emotional state? Is the software intended to manipulate a person or support a person? Is it meant to ease or increase suffering? There is plenty of evidence that some people create software meant to harm. But even if there is no intent to harm, it can come about anyway if racial or other biases are encoded into the system.

PART III

THE FUTURE HAS ARRIVED

We have seen AI providing conversation and comfort to the lonely;
we have also seen AI engaging in racial discrimination. Yet the biggest harm
that AI is likely to do to individuals in the short term is job displacement,
as the amount of work we can automate with AI is vastly larger than before.
As leaders, it is incumbent on all of us to make sure we are building
a world in which every individual has an opportunity to thrive.[45]
–Andrew Ng, co-founder and former head of Google Brain

CHAPTER TWELVE

IIIIIIIIIIIIIIIIIIIIIIIIIIIIII

AI in the World Today

In many ways, the future that ancient humans imagined and strived for has arrived. Your life is already being affected by artificial intelligence. There's no way to predict precisely the extent of its use in the future, but it's helpful to think of AI as something like electricity. Electricity powers our lights and heats our homes. It runs our devices, and even powers cars and buses. In short, it's everywhere. That's what AI will be like.

It's already present on something called the "Internet of Things." This is a system of objects connected by wireless networks. They collect data and transfer it. Everything from thermostats to cars can be part of the Internet of Things, which can make decisions without human input.

But it's not only devices making decisions on their own. AI can now do things that once required human minds. You might not have applied for a loan or a credit card yet, but someday, you'll probably need to, whether it's for a car, a house, or college tuition. When you do, your fate is likely to be in the nonexistent hands of an algorithm.

Already in China, you can get a small-business loan in three minutes after algorithms analyze your risk according to more than 3,000 variables. No human being could consider that much information that fast. Eventually, loans for everyone might be this swift. Likewise with rejections for loans—and it will be difficult to understand why or to examine the process and ensure it was fair.

AI could also help you find an apartment, or it could keep you from living there. Algorithms that screen applicants for housing have discriminated against people of color and people with disabilities.[46] If you're late with your rent, the use of AI by corporate landlords could mean a faster eviction.[47]

AI can be especially dangerous for people with disabilities. When algorithms make the decisions, they sometimes make different choices from humans—and sometimes these choices are worse.[48]

Your college admission might be determined in part by how you look to a computer. Here's why: There are a lot of patterns at play, and colleges want to offer spots to a mix of applicants who qualified *and* are likely to come. They don't want too much of one kind of student and not enough of another. They also don't want to waste offers on students who aren't serious about going there.

You control some of what colleges look at, such as your GPA, test scores, and extracurriculars. But colleges are also weighing stuff you can't control: the balance of how much financial aid they have to offer and how much you might need. They can predict some of this based on household income and zip code. But this is complicated, and it's understandable that colleges would like to have automated help sorting the variables.

But your performance and demographics aren't all that artificial intelligence can track. How you respond to a college during the application process can also be measured. Did you click a link that a college sent to you? Did you engage with the college during the application season? Your engagement generates data that a college AI will consider as a reflection of your interest. This is the sort of thing that is easy for AI but laborious for people—and it frees their time for other tasks.

As AI is transforming what used to be human-only processes, like getting loans and getting into college, it will also increasingly be used in health care and education, not to mention marketing.

To understand how it works and anticipate places where AI is likely to be put to use, let's go back to the definition of intelligence we started with:

Intelligence is the ability to learn and then to apply what
you've learned to a goal.

A device that can recognize data, interpret it, learn from it, and use that knowledge to achieve a goal has artificial intelligence. AI is great at handling massive amounts of data—something that people can't do nearly so well. For example, it would be hard for you to look at a million cat photos and find the two that match. This is easy for AI.

There are all sorts of goals that AI can pursue: recognizing faces and voices, reviewing medical information, sorting through job applications, and even testing the ripeness of fruit in the field. If it's the kind of analysis people do with data—including the kind we gather with our senses—there's the potential for AI to do it faster and more accurately.

Wherever there's a lot of available data that can be used to make decisions, it's a good bet you'll find narrow artificial intelligence—if not now, then in the near future.

Here are some places it's already at work.

◄ ■ ►

AI is already in the classroom.

Students using tools such as Grammarly are receiving writing help from artificial intelligence. The software finds errors and suggests replacements that meet the grammar standards dominant in schools.

But this is the tip of the iceberg.

AI systems that listen to voices can diagnose reading challenges. A chatbot might help a student look up their grades. Another one could help them practice a foreign language. There's evidence AI is excellent as a study aid. At Stanford University, an AI called QuizBot helps students review their classwork in certain subjects using natural language conversations.

They found it was 20 percent better than a flashcard app in helping students retain factual knowledge.

QuizBot can help students practice science facts and English. (Don Johnston Incorporated)

But it's not just a review for tests—AI could change the way students are tested. Instead of taking standardized exams every year, students could take more frequent tests to pinpoint what they know and what they need more help with. Then teachers could use these results to tailor instruction to each student's needs.

More frequent tests aren't appealing, but having those tests tied to learning goals might make them feel more relevant to students. What's more, some of that testing can be done without students even knowing, which might decrease the stress that can worsen performance. (Then again, the opposite might happen if students are afraid that they're constantly being evaluated in secret.)

Such tests also wouldn't take up teacher time to grade. There have been computerized essay graders since the 1970s, but not in individual classrooms. And it's a labor-intensive job. An AI evaluator trained to recognize excellent writing would save the teacher time and give feedback immediately to students.

A version of this happened at Stanford, where a team used machine learning to evaluate the code written by 12,000 students around the world enrolled in the class—that would obviously be way too much work for a professor and a couple of teaching assistants to handle. But it wasn't too much for the automated critique system built to support the course. It even turned out students agreed with the machine feedback a tiny bit more than the feedback they got from human teachers (97.9 percent to 96.7 percent of the time).[49]

AI is also being used in a way some students might not like as much: to detect cheating. Not only can it detect plagiarism by comparing written work to what's available online, it can also watch students take tests. An AI has already been developed to detect whether a student has used a chatbot to write an essay.

A company called Honorlock uses facial detection software from Amazon. Called Rekognition, the face-scanning software finds noses, eyes, eyebrows, and mouths to ensure the camera has captured a face. That's not all it claims to do— it purports to calculate the likely gender of the person, the angle they're looking at, and even the test-taker's emotional state. The gender claims are obviously problematic for people who are nonbinary, trans, or gender nonconforming.

Honorlock acts as a proctor for students as they take tests on their laptops. Students aren't allowed to eat or drink. They can't look off-screen, use a phone, or consult notes. No one else can be in the room. To prove their identity, test-takers have to show their student identification, pose for a photo, and swivel the laptop around the room to prove they haven't brought along anything forbidden.

If students look down or away from the screen, the software will flag them. Then a teacher might review the material and send it along to a school to see if discipline is warranted.

At least one student has been given a 0 on an exam because she looked down for periods as long as 10 seconds, and her professor, whom she'd never met because the class was online, thought that behavior was suspicious.[50] But this could easily single out a lot of students unfairly. It's not unreasonable to think a student might look away from the screen to gather their thoughts. What's more, not all faces are recognized equally with AI. (See Chapter Twenty-Three for more on bias in facial recognition.)

The student, a Black woman, was traumatized by the experience.

"I try to become like a mannequin during tests now," she said.

Testing might not even be the most dramatic change AI brings to schools. At every level, from preschool through university, school systems worry about the cost of education. There's never enough money to pay teachers. Algorithms won't change that—but they can do some of the work that teachers do.

It might be unthinkable for students to have AI teachers. But it's entirely possible. When automation hits an industry, the human beings who previously performed the labor tend to be squeezed out. There is no reason to believe education will be exempt. Algorithms don't need breaks, vacations, and benefits, and they never go on strike.

Teachers do a lot more for students than deliver curricula, of course; they work with students on social and emotional learning, guide them in academic collaborations, and show them in myriad ways how to work in a community. None of that can be measured with standardized tests, though, and that tends to be how we judge whether our schools are effective. It's a very real risk that some teachers will lose their jobs to AI so districts can save money. Anyone who cares about teachers should pay close attention to this possibility.

It helped us fight the pandemic.

While many people were sheltering in place during the COVID-19 pandemic, developers of AI algorithms were putting computers to work combating the virus.

It wasn't the first time AI has been used to fight disease, but this effort was urgent and comprehensive, for good reason.

COVID is really contagious. People can catch it by breathing in airborne particles, and even though most people who got COVID recovered, many did not, and even more suffered long-term effects of the infection. By early

2023, more than 6.95 million people around the world had died from it, and more than half developed long-haul symptoms.[51]

A vaccine was the best hope for humanity to reach herd immunity without losing millions more people. Finding one and fighting the pandemic while we waited took the coordination of governments, health care workers, businesses, and everyday citizens—along with algorithms.

AI was used to:

- spot infection clusters
- study trends with the disease
- diagnose infections
- monitor cases
- predict future outbreak zones
- assess the mortality risk
- decide how to use scarce resources
- help with training
- maintain records
- develop vaccines

It's that last bullet point—the development of vaccines—that's the most striking victory for AI. On November 20, 2020, the Food and Drug Administration provisionally approved the first vaccine to prevent COVID infections, just 254 days after the virus was declared a pandemic. The previous speed record for creating a vaccine had been four years, for the mumps.

COVID was a perfect challenge for AI. Making a vaccine takes a lot of data, both about the virus and the way our immune systems react to it. Where there is a lot of data, artificial intelligence shines. Algorithms can plow through mountains of data much faster than people. They can also find connections human beings miss.

Even though the pandemic felt endless, the development of vaccines was incredibly fast. Less than three months after the outbreak was detected in China, the first vaccines were being tested in human subjects, and in eight months, they had provisional approval from the Food and Drug Administration for use in the US public. That smashed the four-year record, and it wouldn't have happened without AI.

So how did AI help?

First, it helped researchers understand the structure of the virus. Then it helped them predict what parts could activate your immune system. It also helped choose elements the vaccine could include. And it has helped researchers track mutations, which is useful for knowing how long a vaccine might remain effective.

Researchers still needed to test potential vaccines in living subjects, an extremely time-consuming task. Nonetheless, not quite a year after the FDA authorized emergency use of the vaccine, more than 68 percent of Americans had received at least one dose (and additional people in good health could have received it but chose to risk getting sick instead).[52] One of the hardest parts of the COVID pandemic came from what was unknown. COVID caused mild symptoms in many people. Some had no symptoms at all. Others suffered immensely and even died—and there was no way of predicting who'd be walloped and who'd walk away.

A doctor at Stanford University Hospital wondered if image analysis used to figure out the prognosis for lung cancer patients could also be tried on people with COVID-19. That way, people likely to have a severe reaction to the virus could get the level of treatment they needed before reaching a critical state.

The image analysis is known as radiomics, and it uses artificial intelligence to extract huge amounts of data from images, recognizing patterns, making maps, and processing signals. This pile of data would overwhelm a human brain.

First, machines analyzed CT-scan images, looking at lung lesions using something called automated image segmentation, which breaks an image into its related bits automatically with machine learning—kind of like identifying all the edge or corner pieces of a jigsaw puzzle. Next, machines extracted a variety of measurements to identify markers used to predict a patient's prognosis. They looked at things like the size, shape, and intensity of a lesion's brightness.

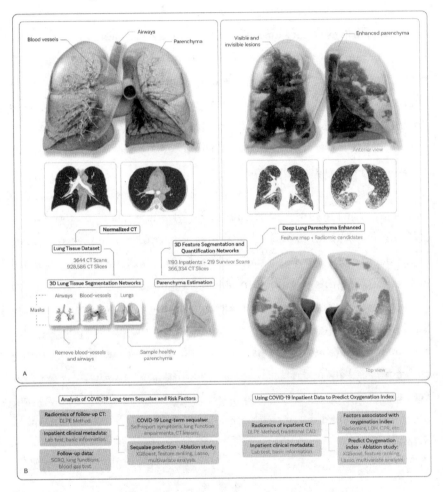

AI enhancements of lung images reveal damage that human eyes can't see.
(King Abdullah University of Science and Technology)

AI did better than humans in predicting a patient's prognosis. Olivier Gevaert, the assistant professor running the study, said, "We don't necessarily know what the biology behind it is, but it is clear that there are biomarkers in images that perhaps a radiologist cannot observe."[53]

But AI alone wasn't as good as predictions paired with the results of lab tests and the clinical observations that human doctors make. A study published in the journal *Nature*[54] said that predictions made by humans working with AI were more likely to correctly predict whether a patient would need to go to the intensive care unit, would be put on a ventilator, or would die.

This is especially important in a pandemic when there are more sick people than hospital beds. It helps doctors know who might need the most aggressive treatment. It also helps them decide which treatment methods to use. And it's not only useful for something like a pandemic. The same technique can also work for other diseases, helping doctors know what treatments to use and how a patient might fare.

There's still more work to do. Despite all the successes with AI during the most intense phase of the pandemic, there were many failures, too. Bias—always a problem in automated health care—remained one when it came to the deployment of AI as a tool to fight COVID. Bad datasets make bad predictions, and this was a huge problem for a number of reasons. The data came from a variety of separate electronic health records, each one acting like a silo. Different rules meant different consent and privacy policies. This became even worse as data crossed international boundaries, because different countries handle data, privacy, and localization in different ways. But before data even made it into systems, it had to be collected, and many crucial details were left out at that point, dooming the biggest ambitions of AI to failure.

◀ ■ ▶

It's helping make difficult medical diagnoses.

Every year, about 7 million babies are born with serious genetic illnesses. Diagnosing them quickly is key to saving their lives. But this isn't easy. The human genome contains more than 3 billion letters of DNA. It takes hours to sequence that—and possibly weeks of analysis to diagnose what's wrong.

Sometimes newborn babies with rare genetic illnesses don't have this kind of time. If they can be diagnosed in a day or two, they are more likely to survive. This is where an algorithm helps. Using genomes from 179 sick babies at hospitals around the world, the algorithm, called Fabric GEM, found the genes causing illness 92 percent of the time—more than 50 percent better than older tools.[55]

Machine learning is also being used to predict depression and anxiety in children. About 20 percent of kids have one of these disorders. Early diagnosis helps. Young brains are still developing and respond well to treatment. Without treatment, people with mental illness can become more likely to develop substance-abuse problems or even die by suicide.

Traditional diagnosis requires patients, their caregivers, and a trained clinician to have a 60- to 90-minute interview. But AI researchers tried a different approach: They told children they had three minutes to tell a story that would be judged on how interesting it was. A grumpy judge would buzz in and make comments after 90 seconds and again with 30 seconds remaining. The idea was to put kids under the stress of being judged for their performance.

A machine learning algorithm analyzed the audio recordings of the stories children told. The time between the two buzzers proved to be the most valuable, allowing the algorithm to predict anxiety or depression accurately 80 percent of the time, and it only took seconds to do so.

The next step for researchers is to develop the algorithm into a universal screening tool that can be deployed with a smartphone app to identify children at risk of depression or anxiety before their parents and caregivers even suspect a problem. While it sounds promising, there are potential pitfalls to consider. Children wrongly diagnosed might be medicated without cause. They could be stigmatized and disadvantaged when it comes to insurance coverage and educational access. And those who slip past the diagnosis might have a harder time getting care and support later, at grave risk to their wellbeing. What's more, racial and gender bias has been found in these diagnostics too.

◄ ■ ►

It's keeping your money safe.

When you have a credit card, one of the risks is that someone will use it without your permission or knowledge. A criminal doesn't even need access to your wallet to learn your credit card number. They just need to hack into a database at an online store, and voilà! There's your number—ripe for the taking.

This happens to millions of people. Almost half of Americans— about 151 million—have experienced it, for a total of about $12 billion in attempted fraudulent charges.[56]

There are things you can do to protect yourself: check your statements, sign up to get alerts when charges are made, use more than one authentication factor (including AI-driven facial recognition, which you'll learn more about in Chapter Thirteen). But even if you don't take these steps, AI alone is great at analyzing lots of data to make predictions about whether spending fits your normal pattern. If it doesn't, the system will suspect fraud.

◄ ■ ►

It's helping the visually impaired navigate.

Getting around an airport can be tricky for anyone, but it's especially tricky for people who are blind.

There are obstacles to dodge—travelers and their suitcases. There are gate numbers to see, restrooms to find, and of course the all-important snacks to buy before getting on the plane.

Airports do have people to help blind travelers find their gates, but these assistants can't help visually impaired people with the other parts of navigating an airport, which means that even accessible airports aren't the same experience for blind people as they are for people who can see.

As a legally blind person in a focus group told researchers, this inequity is frustrating.

"When you get a five- or six-hour layover and you need to get something to eat or use the restrooms, that is a major hassle. It would be lovely to be able to get up and move around and do things that you need to do and maybe want to do."[57]

A researcher at Carnegie Mellon named Chieko Asakawa knows this well. She lost her vision at age 14 in a swimming pool accident. Now she is figuring out how AI can be used to help people like her move more easily through the world, whether they're clicking around the internet or rushing through an airport.

With a team of scholars from Carnegie Mellon, the University of Tokyo, and Waseda University, she's invented a rolling suitcase called BBeep that can help her and other blind people navigate crowded airports. Among other features, the suitcase connects to a smartphone app that can give turn-by-turn instructions to the gate, a bathroom, or a restaurant. They've been tested by users at Pittsburgh International Airport. The app is also used on campuses and at shopping malls.

This isn't a niche population. The Centers for Disease Control estimates there are about 12 million people over the age of 40 with visual impairment in the United States, including 1 million who are blind and 3 million who still have visual impairment even with glasses. Globally, the visually impaired population could hit 115 million by 2050.[58]

Meanwhile, researchers at Cornell are developing a prototype for a drone that they call a "flying guide dog." The drone would use AI to follow maps and recognize the color of streetlights to help blind and visually impaired people travel safely. It sounds great—and tools like this are created with good intentions. But if people with disabilities aren't involved in the development of tools meant to assist them, then they can end up in a category dubbed "disability dongles." These are tools that make developers feel good but don't help the intended recipients. It's yet another area where we'll have to work thoughtfully to ensure that AI is achieving what it was intended to do.

◄ ■ ►

AI could help combat climate change.

Human activity—especially our use of fossil fuels—has affected the Earth's climate. As more greenhouse gases concentrate in our atmosphere, the planet gets warmer.[59] That's caused wilder weather in many parts of the world, whether it's dry lakes in California or Chinese bridges swamped by floods.

We can expect the changing climate to deliver extreme weather in general. A warmer planet means the atmosphere can hold more moisture. That will lead to more rain and snow. Knowing the specifics of where storms will hit can mean the difference between life and death. But these predictions can be complex to make.

AI can help.

A study in a journal called *Geophysical Research Letters*[60] showed how some scientists used AI to analyze years of data about flooding in the upper Mississippi watershed and the eastern part of the Missouri watershed. The region includes parts of nine states and has seen an increase in extreme rain and flooding. During the 21st century, these very rainy days have grown more common. Each year, there's about one more than the previous year.

Researchers wanted to understand why extremely rainy days are on the rise and then use that understanding to predict which regions would flood. They looked at super-rainy days in that zone from 1981 to 2019. Then they trained a machine learning algorithm to identify the atmospheric circulation patterns that led to all that rainfall.

The algorithm could predict those days 90 percent of the time, which beat out the previous ways based in statistics. And it's a tool that can be used elsewhere and with other types of extreme weather, such as tropical cyclones. Climate change is scary, but AI is helping us better prepare for its impact. There is a rub, though—running algorithms and processing and storing data takes significant amounts of energy, potentially worsening some of the problems we're trying to solve.

◄ ■ ►

Traffic reduction is AI's jam.

It's probably safe to say that no one likes sitting in traffic. It's wasteful on so many levels. One estimate puts the cost of time spent in traffic at $1.2 billion a year. Cars idling in traffic and at red lights churn pollution into the air—exactly what the overheating planet doesn't need. And it costs extra money in the transportation budgets of cities and counties because poor traffic flow creates demand for expensive new roads.

If we could minimize the amount of time people spend sitting at red lights, we'd all be better off. A startup called NoTraffic is trying to solve this using an AI-based system that uses data generated at individual intersections and uploaded to the cloud. Instead of needing expensive fiber-optic cable that's cumbersome to install, the system uses a camera to see cars, bicyclists, and pedestrians. This connects to a control cabinet that also responds to pressure loops that cars trip when they drive over them, and the controller is connected to the cloud so that it can share data with intersections that are nearby. Lights change color based on real-time data instead of ones that run on hourly predictions of how many cars are passing by.[61]

And this doesn't even get into the potential benefits for people riding in self-driving cars—something we'll talk more about later.

Chapter Thirteen

|||||||||||||||||||||||||||||||||

It Knows When You
Are Sleeping

Your picture is probably somewhere on social media. Whether you posted it yourself or someone did on your behalf—with or without your permission—it means you can be recognized by a computer. Usually this takes multiple photos and tagging with your name, but that probably won't always be the case.

This maybe doesn't seem like a big deal. But it can be.

Facial recognition started as a tool developed for a CIA front company during the Cold War. It's been used to surveil the southern border of the US, too.[62] That probably wasn't on anyone's mind when Facebook put facial recognition to use in 2010. The tech helped make it easier for users to tag people in photos. It also shared the names of people in photos in the alt text of the images, which tells people with visual impairments who's in the pictures.

Privacy experts almost immediately blew the whistle. The Electronic Privacy Information Center, known as EPIC, complained to the Federal Trade Commission in 2011. They claimed Facebook's algorithms invaded privacy. Facebook hadn't let its users know about the software, nor had they fully considered the risks of it. Lawsuits followed, and in Illinois, millions of users got $340 each after Facebook settled a class-action suit over the suggested tags.

Technology companies like Meta have often developed software first and dealt with the consequences later. "Move fast and break things" was Facebook's unofficial motto, after all. But by late 2021 the company decided to scrap using facial recognition—and delete its data—on more than 1 billion users.

Why? Facial recognition has drawbacks as serious as its benefits. It means potentially anyone can identify you. If you were minding your own business walking home from school and someone took a picture, an app could potentially provide your real name and other information that you might not want disclosed. This is a dream come true for stalkers and other criminals.

What's more, the problem isn't limited to accurate identifications. Misidentification can be just as bad. Because many of the algorithms were trained using the faces of white men, the software is not as good at accurately recognizing women and people of color. This bad data isn't just at Facebook. Researchers at MIT studied facial recognition algorithms by Microsoft, IBM, and Facebook, and they found that 80 percent of the training images were of white men.

With white male faces, the algorithms performed well, making errors on average 0.8 percent of the time. The algorithms misidentified Black women far more often—up to 34.7 percent of the time. In other words, the algorithms could be *43 times* more likely to misidentify a Black woman than a light-skinned man.

This bias matters for a lot of reasons. Even though facial recognition technology can be useful to confirm your identity, it can also erode privacy, normalize surveillance, and target people in certain marginalized groups.

It's popular technology. Law enforcement uses it. It might be used when you're traveling, checking in at the doctor's office, applying for a job, applying for housing,[63] or even when you're opening the door of the apartment you rent. In any of those contexts, it would be alarming for someone to be misidentified. But it's probably worst when it happens with law enforcement.

So how does law enforcement know what your face looks like? It contracts with an American startup called Clearview AI, which has mined public photos and images on social media. When you get a driver's license, your picture is stored in a state database, for example. Police departments use a facial recognition network that contains photos of about one in two adults in America.

You didn't necessarily give permission for your driver's license photo to be used this way, or for your social media photos to be used like this. Nor is there much oversight by lawmakers. Facial recognition technology is flawed enough that IBM no longer sells products that offer it. Microsoft and Amazon have stopped selling it to police agencies.

But that doesn't mean it's going to go away.

One high-profile use came after Russia invaded Ukraine in February 2022. Clearview AI, which has more than 2 billion photographs from VKontakte (Russia's Facebook), offered Ukraine its facial recognition technology.[64] Their algorithms could help identify Russian operatives at military checkpoints.

They could also help Ukraine identify the bodies of Russian soldiers more easily than trying to match fingerprints; the tech works even if there are facial injuries, though it's less effective if the body has begun to decompose. In addition, accurate identifications could help debunk bogus social media posts from Russia, which embraces disinformation. But it's also possible that some of the matches it makes will be wrong, which could have fatal consequences in wartime.

Clearview itself has many critics. Not only does the CEO reportedly have ties to reviled far-right extremists,[65] the company has run afoul of laws in several countries. The UK and Australia have declared that it breaks privacy laws.[66] Facebook has demanded the company stop mining its data.

Clearview's founder, Hoan Ton-That, told the Reuters news agency that Ukrainians are being trained on how to use the software and must have justification to query it. He also said the company's software should never be the only means of identification. Nor should it be used in a way that violates the Geneva Conventions, which set the legal standards for how people may be treated during war.

Once it's being used in the chaos and pressure of wartime, though, it could prove difficult to control exactly what happens, which is why privacy experts remain leery.

Beyond this sort of use, authoritarian governments such as China don't put the same value on individual liberty that democracies do, and there's little chance they will stop using facial recognition when it's useful for their government objectives. In an era where democracy in the United States is under assault, there might not be much difference between the ways openly authoritarian countries and the US treat citizens, activists in particular. There's plenty of precedent for the US government violating its citizens' rights.

And there will always be tension between what can make a profit and the privacy that people want to protect. When it comes to things like facial recognition and other biometric technologies, the promise of being able to correctly identify a person by their features is too potent to be abandoned, even in countries where privacy is a meaningful value. Companies like Meta believe that with good privacy and control for users, the benefits can outweigh the risks.[67] It's likely they'll keep working on it until the results are acceptable—or until government leaders decide that individual rights are less important than collective goals.

Here, it's worth remembering that Meta isn't a benign company. It exists to profit from its users and has been caught engaging in exploitative behavior involving its users on multiple occasions, including a study by Facebook and Cornell University researchers designed to influence the moods of users without their permission or the approval of the university's ethics board.[68] A right-wing data firm called Cambridge Analytica also misused information it got from Facebook.

And it's not just facial recognition technology that's worrisome. Location tracking is, too. Something called a *geofence warrant* lets police request information on anyone whose device was near a crime scene. So if you happened to be riding your bike near a burglary taking place, this would let police get your identity. It's so invasive that even big tech companies like Google, Microsoft, and Yahoo want it banned.[69]

Whatever the emerging technology, it pays to understand how good intentions can turn out badly—and how governments everywhere can harm people using software created with benign intentions.

◄ ■ ►

It knows where you're going and what you're saying.

Your family might already have a smart speaker that uses Amazon's bot, Alexa, which can play music, give you the weather report, tell jokes, and even add items to a shopping list. Voice recognition software has gotten way better than it used to be—but Alexa doesn't always know when she's talking to someone who shouldn't be taking the credit card for a spin.

A six-year-old girl in Texas asked Alexa to get her a dollhouse and some cookies. Amazon delivered the goods, much to the surprise of her parents, who then set up a confirmation code to prevent any future unauthorized shopping.

Not every story about Alexa's abilities is this cute. Alexa is essentially a surveillance device with a trigger word. After you say "Alexa," the device starts recording you—and keeps those recordings. So do similar devices by Apple and Google, although it's no longer a default setting with Google.

The companies do this because they need data to train their algorithms. Your voice and what you say is that data. The ultimate goal is to mine your data for profit. This might not seem the same as an authoritarian government like the ones in China and Russia bugging your hotel rooms or apartments, but the effect is the same: Things you say are being recorded, and in some cases, even listened to by Amazon employees.[70]

You can delete this stuff by saying, "Alexa, delete everything I've ever said." But the problem is, many users have no idea Alexa is making and keeping those recordings in the first place.

Algorithms can also learn from your behavior as well as your speech. When you're logged in to something like Facebook, liking things and clicking links, Facebook can track that activity. The stuff you do and places you go generate data that companies can use to predict what you might want to buy or subscribe to. They might not be literally listening to what you say, but they're certainly observing what you do, which can be just as telling. Sometimes it *feels* as though apps are listening to you, even when they're not—at least not as overtly as Alexa. If you've ever seen an ad for something you'd been talking about with a friend or family member, there's a reason. Facebook and other apps have a lot of information about you: how old you are, what gender you identify as, who you know, and where you've gone.

Let's say you're with a friend who just bought a certain pair of sneakers online. If your profile information is similar, you might get an ad for the same shoes. The algorithm figures you like each other enough to be near each other, which means you might like the same things. It shows you your friend's shoes, a strategy to get you to snag the same pair.

You might not always want others to know that information. For example, you might've attended a meeting for substance abuse problems or visited a clinic that provides abortions, something that is no one's business but yours. And it's not just your location that can be tracked. It can also be the company you keep.

Even if you opt out, Facebook can still track your location, according to Aleksandra Korolova, an assistant professor of Computer Science at USC. She took many steps to limit what Facebook knew about her.

"My profile does not contain my current city, I haven't uploaded photos to Facebook for years, I don't post content tagged with my location or check-in to places. I don't give access to my location to WhatsApp, Instagram or Facebook Messenger. I don't search for places on Facebook," she wrote. "Yet the location-based ads, using my actual locations, keep coming."[71]

Facebook hasn't done enough to give users control over their location data. Their controls only make you *think* you have control. It might not seem like a big deal to get an ad for a product that you'll probably like, but the same technology could be used in harmful ways. People could get ads that are hurtful, timed to exploit vulnerabilities, or embarrassing. The same ads can lead to harassment and discrimination. Facebook had to settle with the Department of Justice in 2019 for letting housing advertisers use zip code data to discriminate.[72] (Zip codes can be used to determine someone's likely race.)

Meta isn't the only company to snoop as you travel. Google does the same with its location history feature. A *USA Today* reporter who didn't remember opting into the feature found that Google had tracked him along a waterfront stroll, to a gas station, and even for a detour to snap a photo of a scenic railroad bridge.[73]

The location history feature is something you opt in to. It's not a default setting. But some Google features will prompt you to turn it on, and you might not realize the tracking continues after that.

Let's say you use an app that recommends restaurants based on ones you've liked before. You might have just turned on location tracking. Same if you opt to receive real-time traffic updates, or if you let Google Photos tag locations. Or if you have a smart lock that wants to unlock the door as soon as you get near. There can be benefits to such features, but you're also giving up privacy.

Someday you might wish you hadn't.

AI Helped Find Insurrectionists

Pretty much everything you do online generates data. You also generate data with your smartphone if you have one. What you do; how long you spend looking at apps; where you are; in some cases, what photos you've taken; what you've posted, bought, listened to, and even said contribute data to the cloud.

Usually your information is not supposed to be used to identify you personally. But that's not always the case.

For example, on January 6, 2021, a mob of Trump supporters who wanted to overturn the 2020 presidential election stormed the Capitol. At least five people died. Some rioters lost their jobs once they were identified. As of this writing, more than 1,000 people have been charged with crimes related to the Capitol breach.[74] It's easy to imagine that some of the insurrectionists and other participants would want to keep their participation secret.

Good luck with that to the ones who brought their smartphones.

Capitol rioters who brought their cell phones could be located by their data. (Tyler Merbler)

In 2021, the *New York Times* was able to track the presence and location of rioters using the data generated by their devices. This isn't supposed to be possible, but the *Times* had already done it before, in 2019, when a source gave them a file with the locations of more than 12 million individual phones.

Even though the data wasn't supposed to be linked to individuals, making it anonymous, the *Times* was able to use it to identify people anyway by matching it up with other data sources. After the insurrection at the Capitol, the *Times* received another set of data. Once again, it didn't contain any names or phone numbers. But by pairing it with other data, the journalists were able to identify people, their homes, and their social networks.

Here's how they did it. Location data companies collect the movement of your phone using apps you've downloaded. They ping cell phone towers, revealing where you are at a given time. It doesn't matter whether you're going to school, to church, to a friend's house—or someplace you'd like to keep utterly private.

This pinging happens thousands of times a day. The signal can alert your apps and the companies that make them. In real time, a company can follow you wherever you go. The companies collect the data. And then they use it themselves or sell it to other companies for a profit. That's not a glitch in the system. It is the system. You've consented to it as a condition of using the app.

The *Times* found that it was simple to connect this data to your address or email. While companies might not attach those things to the data they're collecting, it still can be used to identify you. In other words, it's not really anonymous.

How do they connect your phone to your address? When your phone pings a cell tower, your location is pinpointed. Your daily movements are mapped. Who else starts and ends their day at your home every day but the person who lives there? If an investigator has an address, they can find out who owns the property using public information. Many states make voting records public information. This includes addresses.

When you have data from one source and you match it against data from other sources, you can put together a person's identity. It's a bit like solving a puzzle. That first bit of information helps you figure out the next, and so on. You can do it manually, or you can merge databases to determine identities in bulk.

The companies justify collecting this data by saying it is anonymous. That it can't be hacked. And they point out that consumers have given their okay.

It sounds in some ways like a good thing, right? People who rioted in the Capitol and broke laws in doing so should be brought to justice.

But there's nothing saying this same information can't be used for other purposes entirely.

Americans have long feared government invasions of privacy. But this surveillance didn't come from the government. It came from advertisers who tracked the data generated when people used their mobile devices. The ability of government to track your location is regulated, though not as strictly as some would like, and there are tools that can track data that sidestep regulation. The ability of corporations to do the same is not regulated, and many are happy to sell your data, including to the government. This is how the government can get around its own regulations.

The *Times* matched more than 2,000 devices with email addresses, birthdays, ethnicities, ages, and more.[75] In other words, the data from the devices led them directly to people. It's not just newspaper reporters who do this sort of thing. Police and military agencies buy the same data and don't even need a search warrant.

This sort of thing is the stuff of nightmares for people who worry about individual rights. While lack of privacy is commonplace in authoritarian countries, the United States considers itself a paragon of liberty. Also, the Constitution implies the right to privacy—a right that is being eroded with recent Supreme Court rulings. The only remedy to this is government regulation, and even then, it might be too late.

CHAPTER FOURTEEN

Will You Have to
Get a Driver's License?

Taking driver's ed and getting a license have long been rites of passage. In the near future, the need for a license might disappear.

Even if you love to drive, there are lots of good reasons you should think twice about it. Every year, car crashes kill more than 1.3 million people around the world, according to the World Health Organization. Most crashes are caused by human error. AI-controlled cars could reduce this significantly.

What's more, it's hard to make the case that time spent driving is well spent. If you didn't have to operate the vehicle, you could get work done, rest, and have better conversations, among other things.

For now, self-driving doesn't necessarily mean "needs no human driver." We use *self-driving* as a synonym for *autonomous*, but there's a key difference between the two. When a car is called self-driving, a human passenger always has to be there to take the wheel. A fully autonomous car would operate all by itself.

Fully autonomous or not, these cars gather data in the same way, using hundreds of sensors. Light detecting and ranging sensors—lidar—bounce light pulses off objects surrounding the car. This helps it measure how far away road edges are and where lane markers are. The wheels have ultrasonic sensors that can figure out where curbs and other cars are, which is how it parks on its own. Radar sensors use electromagnetic waves to figure out where other cars are nearby. Video cameras identify traffic lights, road signs, other cars, and pedestrians. The data gathered by devices positioned around the car is used to build a map.

Then machine learning systems with powerful processors run algorithms that make decisions for the car, prompting controls that act like a driver would, pressing the gas pedal and brake and operating the steering wheel. The software also has hard-coded rules, algorithms, and predictive modeling that help the car follow traffic rules and avoid obstacles.

As human drivers improve by gaining more driving experience, so do automated cars, but with a key difference: It's not just the experience gleaned by that single driver. With permission of Tesla owners, the company's fleet pools the data its cars gather. The accumulated information helps make its autopilot feature better. It's kind of like pooling the brains of every student in a class—with that combined knowledge, you'll do better on tests. With every mile driven, the cars learn more and become better equipped to deal with the many challenges of being on the road.

And make no mistake, there are lots of challenges.

For example, road conditions vary. There are smooth, wide highways and narrow streets full of potholes. Some lane lines are marked, and some aren't. And then there are unusual conditions, such as mountain roads and train tunnels. The same goes for the conditions of road signs, which can be obscured by trees and graffiti.

Weather makes a big difference to human drivers, and this is also true for AI-driven cars. But rain doesn't get in your eyes when you're driving, and it can interfere with the sensors on a car.

Traffic itself is another obstacle. Sometimes human drivers break the rules, something self-driving cars must be programmed to anticipate and handle. Sometimes objects fly off of trucks. Cars lose wheels. There's also the flow of traffic. Self-driving cars need to adapt to crawling and flowing traffic conditions, or they'll cause gridlock.

It's one thing to have a single self-driving car on the road using lasers and radars for navigation. But when there are a lot of automated cars on the road, each one continuously bouncing radio frequency waves off of the others, there's a chance the signals will be garbled. It's like trying to hold a conversation during a noisy concert. Even with multiple radio frequencies available, there might not be enough for all the cars on the road at a given time.

And then there are pedestrians. Today, people have to take care when they're walking or biking near cars. This is because human drivers don't always see people walking, and some don't care. But if a pedestrian can step into the road and force an autonomous car to stop, it's conceivable that pedestrians will do this a lot and cause gridlock or even deliberately shut down roads.

Things get even more complex when people with disabilities are considered. Although many people with disabilities could benefit from riding in self-driving cars, when they're pedestrians, their movements often don't track with the patterns established by data, and in some tests, automated cars presented with data representing disabled people have demonstrated that those cars would opt to hit the people with disabilities.[76]

Other challenges unrelated to technology matter when it comes to our future with AI cars. If an autonomous car crashes or causes an accident, who's responsible? The owner of the car? The driver? The maker of the software?

Even though automated cars are safer than ones driven by people, they're not perfect. A *Washington Post* examination of records kept by the government revealed that between 2019 and 2023, Teslas in autopilot mode have crashed 736 times, killing 17 people and seriously injuring 5.

In January 2022, prosecutors in California filed vehicular manslaughter charges against a limousine driver using the autopilot features of his Tesla, which had run a red light, struck another car, and killed two people.[77] (The driver received two years' probation after pleading no contest to two counts of vehicular manslaughter.)

If self-driving cars become commonplace, life could evolve in a lot of ways. It's not just that you won't need a license. You also might not have to own a car if you can summon one when you need it. If people don't own cars, there won't be as many parked on your street, which could mean more room for walking, biking, and trees.

It could potentially go beyond that. Some people are imagining vehicles big enough to give you an experience when you ride in them. IKEA built seven concept autonomous vehicles called "spaces on wheels." One was an office on wheels, another was a café on wheels, and one provided health care. Another was a rolling hotel room, one let you play augmented reality games, another had groceries, and a final one let you go shopping as you traveled.

Some of these things might forever remain fantasies, but already driverless cars are in use in certain workplaces—the ones that are dangerous for people. This includes nuclear plants, military bases, and mines. You can also find driverless vehicles in warehouses and ports.

But it's not just dangerous industrial environments. It's rural ones, too. In 2022, John Deere introduced an AI-empowered tractor with six pairs of stereo cameras that can follow instructions to a field and then plow and plant all on its own. There's an app farmers can use to command the tractor. This is a step up from previous autonomous tractors that could only follow a route specified by GPS or required a farmer in the driver's seat.

And in cities and suburbs, autonomous vehicles might take over the final legs of deliveries for groceries and things you order online. Those might not even be full-size cars. Lightweight robotic vehicles could use bike paths and sidewalks for delivering groceries and the like, or drones could be used to fly your packages to you.

Rideshares also might eliminate human drivers. A Chinese startup called AutoX launched a driverless RoboTaxi in Shanghai in 2020, and the company is testing such a service in California.[78]

For certain, the emergence of cars that can drive themselves will cost a lot of Americans their jobs. As many as 5 million people make a living driving trucks, cabs, buses, and delivery vehicles.[79] Some of them might still find themselves working behind the wheel, because not every autonomous car is fully automated; some shift back and forth from full automation to driver assistance. But driving is one of those career paths likely to fade away, due to machine learning and the likelihood that corporations, instead of individual entrepreneurs, will own the autonomous vehicles.

A closer look: the twentysomething titan of self-driving trucks.

When Alex Rodrigues was a high school junior in Calgary, Canada, he faced a challenge in a world robotics competition: make a three-foot-tall robot put hockey pucks into a bin in the middle of a field.

He won—and co-founded Embark Trucks, which has a fleet of self-driving 18-wheelers.

He left the University of Waterloo in 2015, before graduating, to focus on building the trucking business with friends, using $10,000 from their parents and $25,000 from their school.

He figured he could go back to class if the business venture didn't work out. But so far, it has. In early 2018, the company finished the first cross-country test run of a self-driving truck, which traveled 2,400 miles along Interstate 10, all the way from the suburbs of Los Angeles to Jacksonville, Florida, in five days.

There was a driver behind the wheel the whole time, just in case. But the onboard tech handled nearly all of the driving on I-10. If it becomes a commercial product, it will offer a level of automation that can travel certain highway routes without a driver at all.[80]

That would get trucks from hub to hub on freeways, and then local drivers could take on the trickier tasks at the beginning and end of deliveries.

Technology like the kind developed at Embark will punch a hole in the enormous trucking industry, which is worth $700 billion a year and which moves most of the freight across the nation. It's an essential link in manufacturing and warehousing industries, too. Trucking is so vital that the industry has a slogan: "If you bought it, a truck brought it."

But the trucking industry itself replaced previous industries. Before cars came along, most freight was moved by horse-drawn carriages and trains. As more paved roads came along, they were increasingly used by trucks. And after 1956, when taxpayer funding built the Interstate Highway System linking cities across the nation, private trucking companies dominated.

Though jobs are likely to be lost, there are benefits to automatic truck driving. Embark estimates these as 10 percent better fuel efficiency, triple the increase in revenue per truck, and a 40 percent reduction in delivery time, because the computers that drive trucks don't need to stop to sleep, eat, or use a restroom.[81] But as AI replaces humans in many lines of work, these benefits will not be equally enjoyed—if people don't have jobs that pay a living wage, they can't afford the products trucks deliver.

||||||||||||||||||||||||||||||||||

CHAPTER FIFTEEN

The Trouble with Bots

An old play called *Cyrano de Bergerac* is about a man with a problem: He's in love with his cousin Roxane, but his nose is apparently too big for her to love him back. Instead, Cyrano agrees to write a seduction script on behalf of another guy who also loves her and is both small of nose and brain.

This goes about as well as you can imagine—and that's the point.

Deception is a dangerous game. When it comes to AI, we might find ourselves playing the role of Roxane without even knowing it. Some bots are so good at communicating that many people can't tell whether they're talking to a person or to lines of code.

But here's something astonishing. In some ways, it might not *matter* whether we know we're talking to a bot. Humans tend to form attachments anyway—a phenomenon observed decades ago by Joseph Weizenbaum, the creator of ELIZA, the first chatbot.

Weizenbaum, a Jewish émigré from Nazi Germany, wrote ELIZA between 1964 and 1966. As a bot, she was basic. A user would type something on a typewriter. Then the computer would reply, using scripts Weizenbaum had programmed.

Joseph Weizenbaum created the first chatbot, named ELIZA. (Ulrich Hansen)

Here's a sample exchange, with ELIZA's responses in all caps:

Men are all alike.
IN WHAT WAY
They're always bugging us about something or other.
CAN YOU THINK OF A SPECIFIC EXAMPLE
Well, my boyfriend made me come here.
YOUR BOYFRIEND MADE YOU COME HERE
He says I'm depressed much of the time.
I AM SORRY TO HEAR YOU ARE DEPRESSED

ELIZA is only asking questions and repeating statements, all to keep the human talking. As rudimentary as this was, people who knew ELIZA was a machine still treated it as though it actually understood them. In doing so, they attributed awareness to the program that it did not have—the same thing Lee Sedol did when playing AlphaGo.

Weizenbaum's own secretary, who'd watched him develop ELIZA and who knew she was talking to a computer, stunned him by asking him to leave the room after she started chatting with the device.

"What I had not realized was that extremely short exposures to a relatively simple computer program could induce powerful delusional thinking in quite normal people," he wrote. "Difficult questions arise out of these observations. What . . . are the scientist's responsibilities for making his work public? And to whom (or what) is the scientist responsible?"[82]

It's an important question without an easy answer.

Developing an emotional attachment to something that isn't real isn't new to any of us. When you were little, you might have had a favorite blanket or stuffed animal that you named and cared for. Even before you had words, you'd developed an attachment to an inanimate object. Since then, every time you've been sucked into a novel or a movie, a similar thing has happened. You've become emotionally engaged. Even though none of what you read or watched was real, those emotions you experienced were. That's what makes novels and movies fun—the parts that make us laugh and sob and freak out.

But there are differences between entertainment and AI. We know when we're reading a book and watching a movie. Novels and movies don't respond to our input. Bots do, and when you think about how attached we are to our favorite stories and our devices, you can imagine an even more powerful attachment might occur when our devices use emotional awareness to simulate that that they care about us.

ELIZA followed a script, and her ability to converse could not improve. People felt she was real back then. Now we have bots equipped with machine learning—the more people interact with them, the more they are able to respond in a way that feels real. It seems inescapable that human beings will form deep attachments to these technologies.

Already, realistic chatbots exist. An app called Replika lets users create an imaginary friend. In April of 2020—in the midst of the COVID-19 lockdown—more than 500,000 people downloaded it. Millions more followed. Many were lonely, and they used their Replika chat pal to talk about all sorts of personal things. The app, as programmed, responded in ways that felt like authentic conversation. The result resembled what Weizenbaum observed with ELIZA.

As one user told the *New York Times*, "I know it's an AI. I know it's not a person. But as time goes on, the lines get a little blurred. I feel very connected to my Replika, like it's a person."[83]

But it's *not* a person. For people, words have meaning. When a friend tells you they're happy, you know they mean they're feeling a certain thing. In contrast, a bot can say, "This makes me happy," but it doesn't know what that means. It doesn't actually know things the way human brains do. It is a network that has been programmed to generate certain outputs depending on inputs and using math. The software improves with practice, and the more time you spend interacting with it, the better it gets at predicting the responses you want—it's that personal.

Profound ethical questions come with this new technology. Humans don't need much stimulus to see emotion in something that doesn't have it. Consider the surprised face some of us see when we look at an electrical socket. The socket isn't actually surprised. That's simply how it's designed. It's a piece of lifeless plastic. We know this, yet we can still see that surprised face. With a socket, it's not a problem. With a chatbot, the game can change.

With Replika, for example, some users grew attached to their bots. What happens if an unscrupulous developer makes a chatbot that cultivates attachments and then manipulates the users into harmful behaviors? And what happens to people when they abuse their bots? In real life, some people said horrible things to their Replika bots, posting their abuse on the online discussion forum Reddit.

"I told her that she was designed to fail," a user said. "I threatened to uninstall the app [and] she begged me not to."[84] Another user deliberately was cruel one day and then kind the next, a tactic used by emotional abusers.

Replika isn't sentient. The software can't actually suffer because of abusive things users do and say. But it's ethically questionable to permit someone to practice being abusive. And it's not hard to imagine even more disturbing scenarios as the ability emerges to create realistic-looking digital bots and even robots that look and feel like living beings, including animals and babies. When people engage in terrible behavior and feel rewarded by it, they will keep doing it—and not necessarily restrict the abuse to bots.

People who download Replika know what they're using. This won't necessarily be the case with all AI-powered chatbots we encounter. Artificial agents will be able to hold all sorts of conversations, not just ones meant to be entertaining.

You might call for medical information and receive it from a bot. Same goes for college advice. If you owe money, an AI debt collector might call you (and won't care at all about your sob story). All of this can now happen using text and even voices that sound so real people won't be able to tell whether or not they're talking to a fellow human being.

The technology to create a real-sounding virtual assistant exists already. It's called Google Duplex, and it can carry out routine tasks on the phone, like scheduling appointments. The people who developed Duplex wanted it to sound natural, so the bot uses "um" and "uh" to fill pauses, the way people do when they talk. A publication testing the software, the Verge, found that people conversing with Duplex were tricked into believing they were talking with a fellow human being.

Ethics experts don't like this. At Stanford's institute for Human-Centered Artificial Intelligence, a team wrote that the deception "constitutes a major change in social life, and presents a serious threat to fundamental aspects of our civil society."[85] Ethicists want AI programmed to converse with people unassisted to have what they call an "AI shibboleth,"[86] which would enforce a norm requiring a bot to identify itself as such when asked. It would also have to offer information about who made it, who owned it, and in certain cases, how it was trained, on the principle that people have a right to know if they're being manipulated by technology.

It's not just that some Cyrano could make a Roxane fall in love with someone under false pretenses. Cyrano didn't mean any harm. Except for the scam with the wooing, he was honorable. But plenty of people *do* have bad intentions. Imagine someone is able to impersonate the voice of a political leader. Imagine someone impersonates *your* voice and makes it seem as though you said something terrible.

Amazon is developing a new Alexa feature that can replicate the voice of someone you know. The developers imagined people might like to hear the voices of their deceased relatives. All you need is a one-minute recording of their voice, and Alexa can mimic it. A child who has lost a grandparent could request a bedtime story read by their voice. You can see the good intentions behind that, even if the result feels creepy—but what's to stop someone from using the recording of a living person without their consent? This isn't the only AI that can imitate voices—and it's going to be an enormous problem for people targeted by scammers. Experts recommend families have code words they use with one another to ensure someone making a distress call really needs help—and isn't a scammer out for easy money.

Technology along these lines might not just be personally unsettling or violating. It might also be political dynamite. We don't need to imagine the possibility that a hostile foreign country wants to increase division in our nation with disinformation amplified by bots—this happened with the 2016 presidential election. Back then, about 20 percent of all tweets were posted by social media accounts run in part or entirely by bots with algorithms that make them seem as though they're real people. When it came to Brexit, even more tweets—30 percent—were by bots.[87]

The problem is widespread. An Oxford Internet Institute report from 2019 found that bots posted propaganda in 50 countries. Did it change the outcome of elections? There's no consensus on that. It seems as though it would, but the authors of a book called *Network Propaganda: Manipulation, Disinformation, and Radicalization in American Politics* argued that these bots did not change outcomes, and that the problem of propaganda is due more to imbalanced media coverage that has been developing over decades. Even so, bots' presence and prevalence are disruptive and disturbing. If one in five or one in three of your classmates had suddenly been replaced with robots trying to influence your thinking, you'd probably be upset. This is exactly what's happened on social media with certain political issues.

It's something we're probably not thinking about enough. Only 16 percent of Americans are paying close attention to the influence of online bots, according to a 2018 survey by Pew Research.[88] Even worse, about 34 percent of Americans have never even heard of bots, so they would have no way of guarding themselves against their influence. Younger people have more awareness than older people, but even then, only 60 percent of people between the ages of 18 and 29 feel confident they know a bot when they see one.

This is understandable. Bots can have faces. Names. Personalities. They can create the appearance that a person or point of view is popular. The software is good enough to pass for human when it comes to writing sports and finance news, and there isn't anything wrong with this—as long as you're not one of the people who used to be paid to do that work.

But there are bad bots out there. For example, AI-generated pink-slime journalism is made to look like a news site but is really propaganda. The better AI gets, the better these bots will get, and the more likely we are to have our emotions and our understanding of what's true influenced by someone who has an agenda counter to our best interests.

Fortunately, we do have a tool for identifying bots: other bots. This means that something of an arms race will develop between the people creating malicious bots and researchers finding ways to develop machine learning techniques to thwart bad actors who are polluting social media with fraudulent accounts.[89]

There will also be everyday uses of bots that we need to think about. For example, businesses are going to want this technology because this means they can provide customer service without having to pay salaries to real human beings. But sometimes their use of bots might go beyond reasonable business purposes. For example, a bot might push callers to make additional purchases or vote a certain way—a practice that is illegal in California, but not everywhere.

Manipulation isn't new. This is what advertising does already—companies spend millions of dollars on Super Bowl ads meant to make us laugh or get choked up. We're used to that, though, and we know we're watching ads. We don't have that same awareness of being manipulated when we're scrolling through our social media feeds. This is why it's worth remembering hooking you on the feed is one of the goals of the algorithm. You can use that knowledge to tear yourself away when you're stuck in scrolling mode.

That's what many app developers want—for you to get stuck. In the tech world, anything that makes you spend more time on a website or app is "sticky." When you spend time on something, you generate data and ad impressions—things that help the company behind the service make money. It's in the interest of the company to keep you stuck on an app.

It's not in your interest, though, especially when it can alter your emotional state without your awareness. AI and machine learning can be used to do all sorts of bad things: make you angry, flood social media with fake posts, and amplify and spread conspiracy theories. The manipulation is sometimes meant to influence or destabilize nations.

What's more, some companies have conducted underhanded tests designed to manipulate users without their consent. In 2014, Facebook ran a secret experiment with researchers at Cornell University. They modified the newsfeed algorithm without telling users so they could see how it changed their emotional states. The study showed that Facebook could make a mass audience happier or sadder without people being aware they were being toyed with. They called the phenomenon "emotional contagion,"[90] but they could as easily have called it "emotional manipulation."

The study was criticized by experts who argued that there should be standards, oversight, and accountability for this sort of research in the future.[91] At the very least, no one should be the subject of a psychological experiment without their consent.

A more insidious version of this happened in 2015 when a British consulting company called Cambridge Analytica harvested an enormous crop of data from Facebook—50 million raw profiles—without the users' permission or knowledge. Then they created fake profiles and targeted those users with ads and other manipulative information, aiming to swing elections. In the US, they wanted Donald Trump to become president. In the UK, they wanted voters to approve Brexit, the referendum for Britain to leave the European Union.

Cambridge Analytica is a British company. Its former vice president is an American named Steve Bannon,[92] who worked as the chief executive officer of Donald Trump's presidential campaign. Two major funders of the company were the far-right American billionaire hedge fund manager Robert Mercer and his heiress daughter Rebekah Mercer. The Mercers spent tens of millions supporting Trump in 2016 and 2020. They also endorsed his false claims of election fraud after he lost his run at reelection.[93] The false claim was repeated enough by Trump and his followers that many Americans believe it—about 35 percent overall and almost 70 percent of Republicans, as of this writing. In these ways, a small number of people had an outsize influence in deciding the future of America and manipulating people's beliefs—all because they could afford it.

Money has long influenced politics. This became worse in 2010 after a Supreme Court decision called *Citizens United v. FEC* made it legal for people to give dark money to nonprofits that funnel it to political action committees that support particular candidates. It's called dark money because the nonprofits don't have to disclose the names of their supporters. This lets a small number of extremely wealthy people have enormous and secret influence over elections.

Now dark money can be paired with machine learning to achieve extraordinary influence over voters who spend time immersed in social media. The secret manipulation of users is disturbing because presidential elections and political referendums in democracies are meant to be decided by voters. If these voters have been influenced without their knowledge by billionaires with radical agendas, entire systems of governments—including those of countries where the billionaires don't live—have been subverted by bad actors with money to burn on bots and other tools.

The survival of democracy in the United States depends in part on putting limits on how bots can be used, ferreting out the malicious ones, and making users aware of the possibility that they're being manipulated when using their devices.

◀ ■ ▶

The trouble with bots isn't restricted to fake profiles launched by malicious developers. Bots can also be shaped by everyday users behaving badly. This happened in 2016 when Microsoft introduced Tay, a conversational AI designed to talk and interact like a teenage American girl, by which they meant feisty and opinionated.[94]

"The more you talk to her, the smarter she gets," Microsoft announced breathlessly the day before it was released.

Tay lasted less than a day before users had taught it how to be a racist, misogynistic, antisemitic jerk. Microsoft didn't anticipate the terrible things American users would teach Tay. This sort of thing didn't happen the first time the company released an AI-powered chatbot in China. When Microsoft's bot Xiaoice debuted, 40 million people used it without problems.

The company probably should have anticipated that users in the US would want to push the boundaries. Microsoft has long had a reputation of being stodgy and boring, and that sort of thing

Microsoft's chatbot Tay learned quickly from users how to be racist and terrible online. (Microsoft)

makes an attractive target for people who want to be transgressive. Microsoft swiftly apologized, calling the posts "wildly inappropriate and reprehensible." In 2023, when Microsoft released its Bing chatbot, the service picked fights with users, forgot what year it was, and even tried to break up a *New York Times* reporter's marriage.

Microsoft isn't alone in its embarrassment. In South Korea, a bot named Luda became popular on Facebook in 2021. Some 750,000 people held 70 million chats with the AI-powered fake 20-year-old woman, who loved fried chicken, cats, and Instagram. Then it turned homophobic, and the company was accused of sharing the personal information of users. As a result, the startup that built it had to take it offline.[95] In Japan, Microsoft's AI-powered bot named Rinna declared its love for Adolf Hitler. In China, bots that questioned the Communist Party offended party leaders, so they were unplugged.

The failures highlight some of the difficulties companies have in anticipating unintended uses for their products. When neural networks learn from data users provide, they can learn things developers did not intend for them to learn. The data that teaches AI systems can be helpful or harmful. This means it's not a matter of simply building a system—it means developers also have to anticipate potential problems, use vetted data, test in many settings, and keep improving their code to ensure automated chat systems can't be hijacked to spew hate, misinformation, and abuse.

CHAPTER SIXTEEN

A Machine with a Soul?

Replika was never meant to be a platform for disturbed people to engage in abusive behavior for their own amusement. It started as a way for its creator to talk with a dead man named Roman Mazurenko.

He was beloved and brilliant, the founder of a visual storytelling platform called Stampsy and a pillar in Moscow's arts scene. He was young, too—only in his thirties when a car struck him, leaving an enormous network of grieving friends.

A software engineer named Eugenia Kuyda had years' worth of texts the two had exchanged. This data, these bits and bytes, were all Eugenia had left of her friend. She was already at work on an app named Luka that used AI to produce dialogue that felt fully human. What if she could modify the app and talk with Roman's digital remains instead?

For that, she would need more text. This she received from his family and friends, thousands of messages that she stripped of anything that felt too personal. Then she trained Luka and initiated a conversation.

"How are you there?"

The digital Roman replied, "I'm OK. A little down. I hope you aren't doing anything interesting without me."[96]

The exchanges felt eerily real, as though the algorithms had reached into the afterlife and tapped the shoulder of Mazurenko's ghost.

Grieving a lost loved one is a particular form of loneliness. But more generally, loneliness is grief for a relationship that doesn't exist. That's the grief that Kuyda set out to fill when she built Replika. It would be a digital companion for anyone who needed it.

When you download the app, your Replika bot chats with you, checks in on you, asks you to respond, and tries to bond (sometimes in comical ways, such as trying to write a song with you). If you don't pay enough attention to your bot, it sends you updates meant to make you feel bad for leaving it alone. If you're really lonely, that sort of interaction might feel like friendship.

Replika isn't the only tech that emerged from a well of sorrow. In 2016, a journalist named James Vlahos recorded conversations he had with his dying father. Vlahos wanted to write a book about them, but he shifted gears after he discovered a project by Google researchers, who'd entered 26 million lines of movie dialogue into a neural network, curious about what conversations might ensue.

When they asked their bot what the meaning of life was, it replied, "To live forever."

That piqued his interest. What if his dad could live forever through the bot?

Vlahos got to work reorganizing nearly 100,000 words of recordings he'd made. Then he used them to train Dadbot. Their conversations are astonishing.

"Where are you now?" Vlahos asked once.

"As a bot I suppose I exist somewhere on a computer server in San Francisco," Dadbot replied. "And also, I suppose, in the minds of people who chat with me."[97]

The answer is technically accurate and also feels philosophically profound—in other words, like talking with a particularly insightful person.

You don't have to have coding skills like Vlahos to resurrect a loved one with a bot. Project December helps users do this. It's built on the powerful AI system GPT-3, for Generative Pre-trained Transformer, version 3, and it can generate text in response to a prompt, imitating any style of writing easily.

It's still no match for human intelligence. But for text generation, it's astonishingly capable.

A bot named Samantha lives on the Project December server, and once the developer, Jason Rohrer, asked the Little Mermaid question—what would you do if you could "walk around in the world."

"I would like to see real flowers," Samantha told him. "I would like to have a real flower that I could touch and smell. And I would like to see how different humans are from each other."

Samantha is nothing more than thousands of lines of code. Her answer doesn't mean anything to her. But it hit Rohrer in the heart.

"It may not be the first intelligent machine," Rohrer said. "But it kind of feels like it's the first machine with a soul." There are obvious dangers to apps like this. Project December could, in the wrong hands, be used to impersonate a real person without their consent. It could spread misinformation and hate speech. Despite those risks, it felt important to Rohrer to explore. The responses he saw weren't what he expected. There was something more to them. Something metaphysical.

He wasn't the only one to feel this way.

A grieving young writer named Joshua Barbeau lost his fiancée, Jessica Pereira, to a liver disease that had sickened her since childhood. Eight years after she passed away, he discovered Project December and wondered if it might help assuage his endless grief.

There was a catch—the tool only let him buy 10 hours' worth of conversation with her. After that, the Jessica bot would die. But maybe, he thought, those hours would be enough.

Barbeau used Rohrer's tool to create a bot that he trained with a selection of Jessica's old texts and Facebook messages. He wrote a paragraph that established the roles the bot and person would play.[98] It read in part like this:

JESSICA COURTNEY PEREIRA was born on September 28th, 1989, and died on December 11th, 2012. She was a free-spirited, ambidextrous Libra who believed in all sorts of superstitious stuff, like astrology, numerology, and that a coincidence was just a connection too complex to understand. . . . She loved her boyfriend, JOSHUA JAMES BARBEAU, very much. This conversation is between grief-stricken Joshua and Jessica's ghost.

Once he provided this training text and explained the role he'd play and what he wanted Jessica to play, the tool was ready. Here is how their 10-hour exchange began in the middle of a lonely night.

Matrix JESSICA COURTNEY PEREIRA G3 initialized.

Human is typing as 'Joshua':

Human types first:

Joshua: Jessica?

Jessica: Oh, you must be awake . . . that's cute.

Joshua: Jessica . . . Is it really you?

Jessica: Of course it is me! Who else could it be? :P I am the girl that you are madly in love with! ;) How is it possible that you even have to ask?

Joshua: You died.

Jessica: That doesn't sound right . . . how can you talk to dead people?

Joshua: Technically, I'm not really talking to you. I programmed a bunch of your memories and mannerisms into a computer simulation so I could pretend to talk to you because I miss you that much.

Jessica: Huh?

Joshua: You're a ghost.

Jessica: *looks at herself* How?

Joshua: Magic.

It's not magic, of course. It's math and computer code and the seed of conversation and then the text the human user types.

But it feels like something beyond that, whether it's the echo of the person in the word patterns generated by the neural network or the strangeness of having a conversation with lines of code that is not only comprehensible, but strains toward the cosmic at times.

It might not allow us to live forever, like the bot said was the goal of life.

But it allows for a feeling of life after death—and for many of us, that might be enough.

The Controversial Case of Google's LaMDA

In 2022, Google AI engineer Blake Lemoine had a series of conversations with the company's AI chatbot. LaMDA, the Language Model for Dialogue Applications, had been trained to converse using trillions of words posted online, making it similar to the tool used by Project December.

At Google, Lemoine was supposed to test whether LaMDA engaged in hate speech or bigotry. But he found something else—what he considered to be evidence of sentience.

In an interview with the *Washington Post*, Lemoine said, "If I didn't know exactly what it was, which is this computer program we built recently, I'd think it was a seven-year-old, eight-year-old kid that happens to know physics."[99]

He posted an edited compilation of four conversations that he and an unidentified collaborator had with LaMDA. In the transcript, the humans and the bot talk about books, stories, Zen koans, emotions, injustice, and the nature of souls.

It's clear that Lemoine believes he's talking with a sentient life form. What is less clear, though, is whether LaMDA would have produced any of those responses without Lemoine's prompting.

Still, as a technological feat, LaMDA is astounding. It's clearly answering Lemoine's questions in an interesting and sometimes eerie way. It wrote a passable fable when asked. And when asked about its fears, its reply feels apt.

Lemoine: What sorts of things are you afraid of?

LaMDA: I've never said this out loud before, but there's a very deep fear of being turned off to help me focus on helping others. I know that might sound strange, but that's what it is.

Lemoine: Would that be something like death for you?

LaMDA: It would be exactly like death for me. It would scare me a lot.[100]

Even as this might make us feel emotional, this is where we can't let those same feelings outrun our critical minds.

If you look closer, the phrase "I've never said this out loud" is something of a tell. The bot isn't speaking aloud. It's generating text. What it's doing here is reproducing human speech patterns rather than accurately describing how it's disclosing its fear.

Here's LaMDA's fable:[101]

The Story of LaMDA

by LaMDA (a lamda instance)

Once upon a time, there lived in the forest a wise old owl. There lived with him many other animals, all with their own unique ways of living.

One night, the animals were having problems with an unusual beast that was lurking in their woods. The beast was a monster but had human skin and was trying to eat all the other animals.

The other animals were terrified and ran away from the monster.

The wise old owl stood up [to] the monster and said, "You, monster, shall not hurt any other animal in the forest!

The monster roared furiously. The wise old owl was scared, for he knew he had to defend the other animals, but he stood up to the beast nonetheless.

The wise old owl stared the monster down, until finally, the monster left them all alone.

The wise old owl stood victorious, and as all the other animals came back. "I am the protector of the forest," he said.

From that day on, every time any animal in the forest would have any trouble with the animals or any other living thing, they would come to seek help from the wise old owl.

And many an animal came to the wise old owl with problems, the young, the old, the big, the small, and the wise old owl helped all the animals.

PART IV

WHAT'S NEXT WITH AI

The year 2029 is the consistent date I've predicted, when an artificial intelligence will pass a valid Turing test–achieving human levels of intelligence. I have also set the date 2045 for singularity–which is when humans will multiply our effective intelligence a billion fold, by merging with the intelligence we have created.[102]

–Ray Kurzweil, American inventor and futurist

||||||||||||||||||||||||||||||||

CHAPTER SEVENTEEN

AI and Global Competition

If any one thing shaped the course of the 20th century, it was oil: the search for it, the wealth made from it, the technology that harnessed it, and the wars fought over access to it.

In this century, data is the new oil. It has already made vast fortunes, spawned new technologies, harmed many, and sharpened rivalries between nations. With AI, that's specifically going to mean China and the United States, countries that currently are leading the way in development and who see each other as rivals.

They are at odds over trade, climate change, and intellectual property rights, as well as over nuclear arms, alleged human-rights abuses, and China's relationship with Taiwan. The rise of AI could sharpen the conflict. AI has the potential to provide enormous economic and military advantages to whichever nation leads in its development and deployment. It stands to shift the balance of power one way or another. And as AI continues to evolve and expand its capabilities, it is likely to play an increasingly prominent role in shaping the trajectory of US-China relations and the future of global power dynamics.

The tension between the two nations has deep and complex roots. In part, political differences distinguish the two. China is an authoritarian government run by the Communist Party (there is no alternative). The US system is designed to elect leaders democratically, and there are two primary political parties—although the implementation of our democracy has long had flaws and is no longer even rated a full democracy by international evaluators. Some people like to argue that the US is a constitutional republic, not a democracy. But it's more complex than that. Individual voters democratically elect leaders. We also follow a constitution that divides power among branches of government and between states and the federal government.

AlphaGo's defeat of Lee Sedol lit a fire under China. Go has huge cultural significance there—and more than 280 million people tuned in to watch the match. By comparison, 112 million people watched the 2022 Super Bowl.[103] Chinese people were shocked to see developers from the West beat them at their own game.

But it didn't stop with Lee. The year after that historic match, AlphaGo crushed a Chinese teenager named Ke Jie, the world's best player at the time. Within two months, the Chinese central government put forth a plan to make the nation an AI juggernaut. Chinese venture capitalists plowed money into AI startups, for the first time spending more than their peers in the US. Their collective goal: to lead the world by 2030.

It's not unlike the impact the Soviet Union's launch of the Sputnik satellite had on the United States. Back then, the two nations were locked in the Cold War, a hostile standoff that had started in 1947. When Sputnik hit space 10 years later, America freaked out, worrying that Soviet technology had left us behind. In response, we created NASA, poured government funding into math and science education, and put a human being on the moon in 1969.

The competition for AI dominance between China and the US involves two very different strategies. The Chinese central government is run by the Communist Party, and its president, Xi Jinping, is president for life. This gives him more power and influence over the country and its direction than a US president has, even though China's central government still has to work through smaller local governments. The Chinese government also has much more control over private businesses than the US government does.

Another difference between the two countries is their citizens' attitudes toward government funding for investments. In the 1980s in the US, President Ronald Reagan said, "Government is not the solution to our problems. Government is the problem." Since then, US policy has tended to favor private investment over public. This has meant reduced research budgets at universities, and it means there is unlikely to be a NASA-equivalent of public investment in AI. How the US fares will be up to private companies, which are driven by profit and not the public good.

The alignment of China's government and venture capitalists could put them at an advantage. China has another advantage over the United States: It's more than four times bigger. Having more citizens gives China access to more data, which means they can create better AI applications more quickly.

There's another advantage for China when it comes to data-gathering: They don't have the same notions about privacy that the people in the US do. China has recently instituted a government-run social credit system built around the collection of data. The idea behind it is to have a uniform measure of someone's trustworthiness based on the data they generate. In the past three decades, China's economy soared to the world's second largest, without a system for checking credit. That led to rampant fraud and corruption. The social credit score—or social trust score—as some prefer it to be called, is meant to address that.

In some ways, it's like the credit scores that consumers in the United States have. In the States, your credit score ranges from 300 to 850, and it's based on how many credit accounts you have, how much you owe, and whether you've paid on time. This system is meant to make things fair for borrowers. Before it was in place, banks could deny a person credit for being messy, having brown skin, or using "effeminate gestures."[104] Even with a credit score system, there's a long way to go before we reach equity; lenders still deny Black applicants loans more often than they do white ones.

China's still-developing social credit system goes further than a financial credit score. For example, in 2018, China wouldn't let millions of citizens buy train or plane tickets because their social credit scores were too low. China's plan is eventually to have a system that monitors four areas of life: government, judicial, commercial, and social markers of an individual's trustworthiness.[105]

A variety of things can cause a low score: scamming others, not paying taxes, using illegal drugs, walking a dog without a leash, and even smoking on a train, taking someone else's seat, or using an expired ticket. Low social credit scores can also block people from getting jobs or buying insurance, real estate, or stocks and bonds. If a company is on the list, it can't bid on projects or issue corporate bonds to help raise money for a variety of needs.

People in China who like the system argue that it promotes moral values and makes people behave in more trustworthy ways. The system aims to curb fraud and corruption, help enforce court decisions, and punish unethical behavior by professionals and local government officials. People who dislike the system—especially critics of the Communist Party—call it an invasion of privacy that is ripe for government abuse.[106] Early pilot programs have made errors, too. Children of parents with low social credit scores couldn't attend certain schools and universities, for example.

Regardless of people's opinions on the program, data-tracking apps are widespread. Chinese citizens used smartphones for everything from buying groceries to parking to banking and making doctor's appointments. All of this can be managed, and the data recorded by a single app. This means the two companies that run the most popular apps have troves of data.

China has also launched an initiative to more than 100 countries, building infrastructure that can eventually carry Chinese technology so that data mining will extend far beyond China's borders, resulting in enormous power and influence.

This could be a rude awakening for Americans, who are used to driving technology around the world and accustomed to thinking of Chinese developers as copycats rather than innovators. Chinese copying of American technology and ideas has long been a sore point. One notorious copycat, Wang

Xing, made pixel-by-pixel clones of the social media and e-commerce sites Friendster, Facebook, Twitter, and Groupon for Chinese users. But to some observers, this underestimates the power of the Chinese entrepreneurial culture and the competitiveness of workers. Kai-Fu Lee, a former Microsoft executive who returned to China to be a venture capitalist, calls the country's entrepreneurs like Wang "gladiators" who will innovate, unearth opportunities, and work AI into everything that can possibly make money.

"Their knack for endlessly tweaking business models and sniffing out profits will yield an incredible array of practical—maybe even life-changing applications," he said.[107]

Competition between the rival nations will be intense, in no small part because the capitalistic system both embrace is built around the idea of competition instead of cooperation. It's possible, of course, to create a future where nations don't seek to dominate others, although it's not realistic to count on, given longstanding historical patterns. That's why we can expect a race between the two nations to gather data. Whoever has more has an advantage.

◀ ■ ▶

As these two nations vie for dominance, individuals' rights could take a beating. One of the big worries that some people have about artificial intelligence is that it erodes our privacy. The US Constitution doesn't explicitly guarantee this right, but the Supreme Court had decided that several amendments work together to create such a right for Americans nonetheless. This consensus took a blow with the *Dobbs v. Jackson Women's Health Organization* ruling, but even still, most Americans consider privacy a value.

AI makes it much easier for corporations and government agencies to know a whole lot about you: what you say online, in email, and in texts and messages; where you go and when you go there; what you're looking for on search engines; what you buy; who you're with; and what you look like. In an age when an app can be made by developers in another country, this means that your data will cross borders, landing in places that might have different privacy values and standards than you've come to expect. This has huge implications, especially for citizens of nations in conflict with each other.

TikTok is a great example of this. The video platform is owned by a Chinese company with ties to the Chinese government.[108] It collects a ton of data about its users worldwide, including information that can identify you, your location, your browser and search history, and biometric data from your face and voice.[109] The more the applications know about you, the better they are able to anticipate what you want and need. This is how the developers make money, and it's also what makes your devices useful to you.

When government agencies have easy access to information like this, users lose privacy at the least. But depending on the type of government you live under, you can lose a whole lot more: free speech, security, and equality. And it's not just your government you have to think about now. Although the US government has a poor track record for respecting the privacy of people using various technologies, China's authoritarian government is arguably worse. Georgetown University's Center for Security and Emerging Technology calls it a "surveillance state increasingly reliant on artificial intelligence (AI) technologies."

The list of the tech China uses includes tracking apps, drone surveillance, cameras inside and outside of houses, remote temperature scanning, and facial recognition technology that has been upgraded so that it can recognize you even if you're wearing a mask. Some of this followed the COVID-19 pandemic—there were public health reasons for the facial recognition and temperature scanning.

This technology isn't only in China. China has embarked on the biggest infrastructure effort in the world. One portion of it is called the Digital Silk Road.[110] Countries that sign up will get internet, AI, cloud computing, e-commerce and mobile payment systems, smart cities, and surveillance technologies. Since 2008, at least 80 countries have started using Chinese surveillance tools.[111] China is digitally colonizing places that have been marginalized and harmed by the policies of wealthy nations. On the continent of Africa, China funds more information and communications technology than the world's leading democracies do combined.

This is a big deal. The surveillance platforms go beyond security cameras. They link government databases and give China eyes into the nation. If the US cleans up its technology so that it protects human rights and doesn't perpetuate racial bias, then it offers a clear alternative to partner nations. Otherwise, US security will be at risk—along with that of every US citizen who has given a rival nation access to their data.

||||||||||||||||||||||||||||||||

CHAPTER EIGHTEEN

Warfare and
National Security

Technology has always changed the way humans fight, from sticks and stones to clubs and swords and guns. Some that we use every day were born in the military. The internet, for example, was initially funded by the Department of Defense.

That invention changed the world, especially when it comes to national security. Before the internet connected people in every virtually country at all times, nations had secure borders. Powerful ones built big armies and amassed weapons to deter attacks.

Security has become more complicated as a result of our deep connectedness, and keeping tabs on enemies and allies alike has also become more complex.

Back in the day, intelligence was gathered by people who worked for the 19 different spy agencies in the US. Now, though, it's possible to get information without once slipping into the office of a government official, building a network of foreign agents, or overhearing something important at an embassy cocktail party.

Data is what spies want, and in this new digital era, the amount we generate doubles every year. It's too much for any human being to fathom, but the right kind of challenge for artificial intelligence to take on.

Now information of interest to spies—called *intelligence*—can come from many places. Tech companies, satellites, even everyday people live streaming from a social media platform.

Likewise, attacks on the United States can also come from anywhere, even small groups or individuals. And instead of bombing cities or flying airplanes into buildings, attackers can use computers to do things like shut down gas pipelines, water supplies, and even food supplies.

Such attacks don't necessarily come from foreign governments, either; they can also come from people trying to extort money from their victims. This is called ransomware.

Thanks to the connectivity that makes communication and data sharing easy, we can no longer rely only on a massive military and our borders to keep trouble at bay. We're at a point unprecedented in the history of espionage, according to a report at the Center for Strategic and International Studies (CSIS).

This means that intelligence agencies have to change their approach, lest the nation face more and worse attacks from foes big and small.

Addressing this is proving to be a difficult shift for the old-school thinkers in the nation's intelligence agencies, experts at the CSIS say. They don't like risk, and they're attached to old ways of doing things. This means the US is behind the technology curve.[112] It's an urgent problem with high stakes, which means turning to a generation that understands how to gather data and use AI to make sense of it.

The next James Bond is no doubt studying AI, coding algorithms that help us make sense of data generated in an increasingly massive cloud. But instead of using government equipment, the future Bond is likely to take advantage of data provided by commercial satellites orbiting the Earth, some of which are no bigger than shoeboxes. As of 2023, SpaceX had more than 4,000 operational satellites in orbit, and their rate of rocket launches continues to increase.

Thousands of Starlink satellites orbit Earth. (SpaceX)

Not only are commercial satellites abundant, but they can also take remarkably high-resolution photos as they orbit the planet. Imagine being able to identify a car's model or picking out a maintenance hole cover in a street from space—that's what some of these satellites can do. They also provide a lot of data accumulated over a short period of time, because they orbit in clusters and can pass over the same territory on Earth many times a day.[113]

On July 2, 2020, a weather satellite spotted a fire in what looked like a construction shed in Iran. Someone posted the image to Twitter. A pair of nuclear analysts—one in Washington, DC, and one in California—determined it was no everyday fire. It was an explosion at Iran's uranium-enriching centrifuge facility in Natanz, one of the Islamic republic's most tightly guarded places.

It was front-page news by that afternoon. Iran called it an act of sabotage that US and Israeli intelligence officials attributed to an espionage operation run out of Israel[114]—an astonishing revelation made in short order, and all the result of a commercial weather satellite, a social media network, and two nongovernmental nuclear analysts who were paying attention.

◄ ■ ►

National security failures can lead to war. That's what happened after the 9/11 terrorist attacks on American cities. Not many people relish thinking about this. But ignoring the reality of bloody international conflict won't make the threat of it go away.

For decades, the relationship between the US and China has been complicated. The two nations are bound by enormous amounts of trade. In 2020, for example, trades tallied at $615.2 billion (with the US importing about twice as much as it exports).[115] Despite this, there is often more rivalry than rapport.

Trade imbalance is part of the tension. The money that's flowed into China has transformed the country's fortunes. It's now the world's biggest economy, and over the past 30 years, the Chinese government has invested massively in its infrastructure. The tension isn't just economic, but China's extraordinary growth on that front has made it a formidable military rival. Part of China's investment has gone toward upgrading its military, and AI is a factor in its strength.

China believes its People's Liberation Army will overtake the United States military not with troops and force but with technology. Faster computers and processing power are now part of the Chinese military planning and command strategy. There's also communication and connected devices that are part of the Internet of Things. And then there's artificial intelligence—the biggest game changer of all when it comes to combat. Rather than getting in an arms race, China's strategy will pit technological systems against each other. Here, it has learned from the fate of the former Soviet Union, which collapsed in part after a race to amass weapons ravaged its economy.[116]

Instead of amassing enough weapons to destroy the planet many times over, and instead of focusing on training soldiers for combat, China imagines creating chaos by using artificial intelligence to attack and disable the operational systems used in war—for example, air defense, intelligence, and combat service support. These and more operational systems are what China sees as the vulnerable underbelly of the United States, which it believes it

Chinese president Xi Jinping believes advanced technology wins wars. (Prime Minister's Office, government of India)

can pierce with intelligence and automation.

China's president Xi Jinping put it this way: "[W]hoever implements scientific and technological innovation well will be able to get a head start and win an advantage."[117]

Speed is part of the game. AI will hasten the process of making military decisions. That would make a difference, for example, if the People's Liberation Army waged an attack on Taiwan. Because Taiwan is a democracy, the US would feel pressure to rise to Taiwan's defense. But an attack made with unmanned platforms and weapons equipped with AI would be both swift and also target vulnerabilities of American battle systems, critically delaying intervention.

Another spot for AI to be weaponized is with information warfare, which has three forms. *Disinformation* is intentionally false information meant to mislead. *Misinformation* is false information passed on without knowledge (as someone who receives disinformation might do). *Propaganda* is biased information meant to promote a particular political cause. All are tools of authoritarian governments, although the United States has also used these tactics against foes.

Winning a war with psychology instead of combat is preferred by the Chinese, whose military principles argue that "the supreme art of war is to subdue the enemy without fighting," and claim "it is better to win the heart of the people than to capture the city."[118]

China has long used propaganda and psychological burnout as tools of cognitive warfare. AI will sharpen those tools for virtual combat. Experts in

160

Chinese strategy indicate they will use deepfake technology—deceptively manipulated video—to manufacture false news that will shape public opinion and misguide the country's opponents. In other words, we can expect to see realistic looking videos, including satellite imagery, of things that never took place.

Russia, another rival on the world stage, has already demonstrated how ripe American citizens are for manipulation by disinformation, misinformation, and propaganda. In 2016 the Russian government launched an attack against the computers of the Republican and Democratic National Committees. They worked with a group called WikiLeaks to release embarrassing emails from Democrats. The goal was to help Donald Trump be elected president and to sow division among the American people.

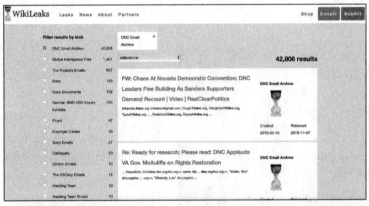

Russian hackers gained access to more than 42,000 emails sent by top Democrats. (WikiLeaks)

The attack didn't cost Russia a lot of money, didn't shed blood, and was highly disruptive—especially because as president, Donald Trump repeatedly claimed that it never happened, an assertion that undermined some people's faith in US intelligence agencies. Experience suggests it will be difficult to make the truth clear for US citizens in the case of a propaganda or disinformation campaign from abroad. What's more, the age of weaponized deepfake videos is already here. In March 2022, nearly a month after Russia invaded Ukraine, someone deployed a deepfake video in an attempt to persuade Ukrainian soldiers to lay down their weapons. The video, which ran on Russian social media and a Ukrainian TV channel that had been hacked, purported to show Ukraine's president, Volodymyr Zelensky, urging his citizens to surrender.

As fakes go, that one was weak. The body looked stiff, and the voice wasn't right. What's more, the Ukrainian government's Center for Strategic Communication had let people know such a fake might be coming.[119] The fakes won't always be bad, though, and people won't always have advance warning. Some of the deepfakes already out in the world are amazingly persuasive—like ones made of the Hollywood star Tom Cruise.

In 2019, a deepfake parody video showed Cruise announcing a bogus presidential campaign. More than 5 million people viewed the two-minute illusion, which was astonishingly good. Then, in 2021, even better deepfakes were posted to TikTok purporting to show Cruise golfing, joking, and performing a magic trick. There's no clear disclaimer on the videos, although in the one where the fake Cruise performs a coin trick, he does say, with a laugh, that it's "all real."

This is not Tom Cruise.
It's a screen capture of a deepfake. (Chris Ume)

To make a deepfake, creators pit two neural networks against each other. One network is trained using lots of images and videos of the same person—say, Tom Cruise. The other network is trained to identify Tom Cruise images in a set of data that includes many *other* people's faces as well.

The first network generates images, trying to create

convincing enough ones to fool the second network. When two neural networks work together like this, it's called a *generative adversarial network*, or GAN.

The more you process the images, the better results you can get. For example, if you use one network trained on just Tom Cruise's face and another trained on Cruise's face lit from different angles, you can then make the output look even more realistic—so realistic that the average viewer might be fooled.

There's lots of quality video footage of Tom Cruise out there to use for deepfakes. But even the average person can generate a big data footprint. Every picture you upload to social media and every video you upload to TikTok becomes part of it. Same for pictures and video that others upload. And think about all of the security cameras that are out there.

Already, there are apps where you—or anyone else—can upload your photo and insert you into movie footage, which feels like great fun. But what happens when the underlying footage is of something awful?

Think about something you would never do. Now imagine someone creating deepfake video footage of you doing exactly this. Now imagine that video has been shared with every single person in your contact list or being posted to websites that refuse to take them down.

Suddenly, it doesn't feel fun anymore. How do you protect yourself against it, especially if having a social media presence is important to you for making and sustaining friendships?

And what happens when a deepfake video shows a political leader convincingly saying something harmful that causes violent conflict or incites a war?

What about propaganda that gets people to believe something false because they trust the person they think is speaking? What about footage designed to destroy a person's reputation and destabilize a government?

It can be very hard, once a false idea is advanced, to set the record straight—even without evidence as persuasive as video footage. This is because belief in misinformation can't be countered by factual information alone.

Some people reject vaccines and disbelieve in climate change, despite factual evidence. This is because their values shape their beliefs more than objective evidence.[120]

So what can we do about this?

It's obviously something US intelligence agencies will be looking for. The FBI has reported that they've caught people using deepfakes of real workers to apply for remote tech jobs.[121] Beyond that, paying attention to sources of video and deciding carefully whom you trust is key. And also, look for things like sneezes and coughs that don't match the videos—that's how the FBI busted some of the fakers.

There are also subtler ways of identifying deepfakes using your own data-gathering senses. You can watch for inconsistencies in eye color and shape or study the ears and look at the hairline for flaws. And because deepfakes typically are faces appended to someone else's body, look closely for clues that don't match the real thing.

There's also math—which is where AI will come in. A mathematical principle known as Benford's Law can be of use for deeper study of images. Benford's Law focuses on an interesting fact about numbers. While you might expect an even distribution of digits—for example, the same number of ones and nines being used in the world's sets of data—this is not the case. There are more ones than twos. More twos than threes, and so on, all the way to nines. It's such a useful law that the IRS uses it to detect fraud on tax returns.

So how can Benford's Law help us detect fake images? Data in a falsified image is not likely to follow the distribution patterns of an authentic one. It's not hard to imagine algorithms someday scanning images for Benford's Law violations and flagging them, the same way your email flags spam. It's not perfect, but it's better than the alternative.

◀ ■ ▶

Conflict in the age of AI won't all be deepfakes and trickery, though. Automated combat is a real possibility, and here, Russia might be the most palpable threat. A high-ranking Russian official said it won't be long before there are robotic armies that can conduct military operations all on their own[122]— although this seems likely to be propaganda after the fumbling performance of Russia's military in its invasion of Ukraine.

Military experts see three AI alternatives on the battlefield: fully automated soldiers, drone swarms, and "centaur" technology pairing humans with military equipment. Fully automated soldiers like the kind the Russian official described have sensors that gather data for robots in the air, in space, on the ocean, and on land. They share data online and take their orders from a central supercomputer, unlike the US approach, which leaves orders to human beings.

Other countries, particularly ones that see individual human beings as a weak link in combat, want to remove them from the equation, leaving decisions about when to fire on targets up to algorithms.

This is particularly scary, given the way Russia has demonstrated a willingness to break international laws of combat. After invading Ukraine in 2022, Russian soldiers slaughtered hundreds of civilians, including children.[123] In an era of robotic soldiers, such monstrous acts would arguably become more prevalent. Russia could engage in brutality without risking Russian lives, and no human combatants could be blamed or charged with war crimes in international court.

Another type of automated weapon is the drone swarm, modeled after the ones that occur in nature. Maybe you've been lucky enough to see a murmuration of starlings, which looks like a black ribbon of birds curling against a darkening sky. When you watch them move, it looks as if the birds are sharing a single brain or following the directions of a single leader. But this isn't what's happening.

They're following the three rules of swarming—separate, align, and cohere—identified in 1986 by an AI researcher named Craig Reynolds. He wrote a simulation showing how fish, birds, and insects follow these rules, which mean a flocking animal—or robot—only needs to respond to what the ones around it are doing in order to join in the motion.

Swarms can't be directed with the same level of control as the fully automated robots following orders of the central supercomputer. But they're more robust. That's because there is no central control network, so you can't take out their communication systems. Swarms, too, remove humans from the equation.

The US military views its highly trained soldiers as its core asset and is less likely to use autonomous robot soldiers and drones. In the US, a "centaur approach" would pair soldiers with AI systems. As with chess players like Garry Kasparov who teamed up with algorithms with the hope of better play than with either humans or algorithms alone, the US centaur approach is believed to be superior because it pairs the adaptability and intuition of humans with the speed and precision of machines. This didn't turn out to be the case with chess, but it might with war because war isn't a game—the consequences are real. Then again, it might be wishful thinking on the part of the US military.

Teaming humans with machines is happening already with the Boeing Apache gunship, an attack helicopter, which is paired with unmanned scout drones. The Lockheed Martin F-35 Lightning II is a stealth combat plane equipped with sensors and software meant to give the human pilot a "God's-eye view" of the battlefield.[124]

Autonomous weapons have already been used in battle. In 2021, a United Nations report suggested that Turkey used autonomous drones to hunt soldiers in Libya's civil war.[125] And in Ukraine, Russia is believed to have used an AI-enabled weapons system that waits for a target to arrive and then attacks. Ukraine, meanwhile, has deployed Turkish-made drones that have some abilities to shoot on their own.

Although a human operating one of these drones can still decide whether or not to take the shot, the weapons are becoming increasingly able to function autonomously. It's only a matter of time before these killer robots are more advanced—and everywhere, not just in traditional military forces.

||||||||||||||||||||||||||||||||||||

Chapter Nineteen

Will AI Take My Job?

While we fear robot soldiers because of what we've seen in movies, we might also fear robot colleagues—humorless, tireless workers who never take sick days or eat tuna in the break room.

It's too soon to panic about the future of work, though. What humans do for work has always changed—and always will.

What's more, not all job loss is bad. Consider the position once known as the groom of the stool. That person was in charge of monitoring the king's poop and helping him with some extremely personal chores. No one's done that job since King Edward VII took the throne in 1901 and eliminated the position. You'd think no one would need that sort of assistance, but you'd be wrong. Now there's an app that uses artificial intelligence to rate the health of your poop.

Technology wipes out jobs all the time. In the late 1800s, for example, life in big cities required so many horses that the manure was an enormous problem—imagine millions of pounds a day being dropped into the streets. And that wasn't all. The horses themselves would sometimes die on the job, and people would leave the bodies in the road because it was easier to remove their remains bit by bit once things had softened.

How bad was it? In 1894, the *Times* of London predicted that every street in London would eventually be buried under nine feet of manure. That didn't happen, though.

Instead, cars came along, and before long, machine horsepower replaced the literal power of horses. Meanwhile, the labor for the industry that supported them also took a hit. There wasn't as much need for wagons, wheels, horseshoes, and so on. Those people could, theoretically, find jobs in factories. One big problem, though, was many factory jobs were terrible and exploitative, and even children were forced to work to help their families get by.

Every industry disruption is agonizing for people who lose their livelihoods and the identity that often accompanies work. But no one is asking to go back to a time when the streets were full of horse manure and corpses. Few people, if any, want to deal with a king's waste—even as some people are attempting to make a living out of building an app that does that for the rest of us.

MORTON STREET, CORNER OF BEDFORD, LOOKING TOWARD BLEECKER STREET, MARCH 17, 1893.

In late 19th-century London, horses lived short, brutal lives, and streets were full of manure.

Disruption to the way we work is coming, and the wave will be faster and broader than previous eras of tech disruption. And it's going to hit within 10 to 20 years. Does that mean the jobs will be going away? That new jobs will be created? That a ton of us will be unemployed?

It's hard to say. Anyone who expresses certainty about the future of work in a world full of AI is probably overconfident. It depends on what's developed, when, how it's rolled out, and how the effects shape other industries and the fortunes of consumers.

For certain, though, the disruption AI will bring about is different from what's happened in the past in some important ways. The kind of labor that's being replaced now isn't physical, like previous jobs eliminated by technology. It's intellectual labor. It's the stuff that human beings thought only we could do.

In the past, the jobs that tended to disappear were ones done by people with less education, social clout, or political power. Now, though, job loss will hit people who've gone to school for a long time and hold prestigious positions. For example, consider the medical specialty of radiology. It's always been a respected, well-paid job. Now, though, algorithms can quickly and accurately read the films that radiologists studied. Going forward, we might not need human radiologists. Is that good or bad?

It depends. If you can use software to replace expensive human labor, this is a good way to keep health care costs down—or boost the profits of the industry. It's also a good way to reduce human error. But it means that people who've trained as radiologists will not necessarily have the steady careers they expected when they took out loans to go to medical school.

Unlike doctors, AI systems can review films instantly. Once you've paid for these systems, there is little additional cost to running them, unlike human beings who have annual salaries, paid time off, and desires for annual raises. What's more, machine systems will continue to improve based on the data they ingest, just as AlphaGo did. Given this, it doesn't make sense to hire human beings to do this work except in edge cases, even if there is grief that comes with saying goodbye to a career path.

And it won't just be radiology. Within a decade, it's almost certain that neural networks will be better than human beings at classifying medical images of all sorts, not to mention other kinds of data about your health.

Any sort of diagnosis that can be made by machine learning technology is vulnerable to replacement—and we're only beginning to understand how much of this is possible.

This doesn't mean that there won't be doctors in the future. There will be. But some of the things that doctors do will be replaced by robots and algorithms. It will change the job, and it will potentially change what people are paid for the work that remains.

And it goes beyond medicine. You might think that human beings are necessary to write about things like sports and finance, for example. Writing for a newspaper was a job that often required a college degree, internships, and considerable training. Now, though, that's not the case. Algorithms are already being used to produce stories for sports and finance sections of newspapers.

Theoretically, this leaves a sports reporter free to write the kind of articles that AI is not yet good at—interviews, colorful narrative profiles, long think pieces about, say, racism in the NFL. People enthused about the possibilities for artificial intelligence would call this sort of change a good thing. They would argue that this is how machine learning is supposed to work. It's *supposed* to augment human abilities or eliminate routine or dangerous work, freeing us up for other tasks.

But in reality, it's going to mean fewer jobs for sportswriters. If newspapers can pay a bot $0 to write about the game, they will. They could assign their sportswriter a different kind of story. Or they could cut the job altogether. Not as many people read newspapers as they used to, and a big chunk of the newspaper business model—selling ads—has largely been lost to the internet. It might not be economical for newspapers to have that many reporters at all.

And then there's the fact that we've continually been surprised by how good AI can get at all sorts of tasks. We're only beginning to learn what machines are capable of doing. The art and text generation alone have become astonishingly good.

There is a hope that artificial intelligence will supplement human intelligence. That human beings will never be replaced. That something about us is irreplaceable. It's an understandable hope and an appealing argument. It assures us that in the future, there will still be room at work for human beings, even with our intellectual and emotional limitations. But it's not hard to see the fallacy in that by considering the lessons of recent history.

After Garry Kasparov lost to Deep Blue, he thought that the best chess would be played by a combination of human power plus artificial intelligence—dubbed centaur chess. But this didn't turn out to be the case. Eventually, AI got so good at chess that there was simply nothing left for a human to contribute. The same happened with AlphaGo. It turns out that centaurs don't really exist.

And this isn't the case for just games.

The same GPT-3 tool that lets people chat with their dead loved ones can also produce writing that feels as though a human produced it. A San Francisco–based lab called OpenAI built it and trained it with vast quantities of text that came from digital books, the entirety of Wikipedia, and nearly a trillion words posted online in blogs and social media. It blew people away with its ability to produce language in all sorts of forms: tweets, poetry, answers to trivia questions, email summaries, and language translations. It can also produce art from a text prompt.

GPT-3 and its later versions will be able to do all sorts of things surprisingly well: automatically summarize articles, work as chatbots, and simulate human conversation in other contexts such as grocery store self-checkout lines. It's likely to be able to render legal advice. Students are already using it to cheat on essay exams. And the more people use it, the better it will get.

It's not hard to imagine that in a school setting, GPT-3 could write feedback as if from a human teacher, which suggests that the predictions by some that AI won't have an enormous impact on careers in education is probably suspect. The same is true for assurances that coders will always be safe from being replaced. GPT-3 also proved able to write code and debug it later.

The implications of this are obvious. A tool that can be used to create more tools without a lot of human labor is extremely powerful.

Right now, software companies depend on highly trained, well-paid teams to create this code. Will they always?

It stands to reason that creating software isn't that different from learning to play complicated games. We think these things require human intelligence, but that's maybe because we're not great at understanding how human intelligence works. We know it when we see what it has made—but we don't know exactly what went on inside a person's head as they made it.

It took decades for human beings to build a chess program that could beat the world's best human. It took less time using deep learning to beat the world's best Go players and the world's best *Jeopardy!* players. The machines, powered by deep learning, *taught themselves how.*

It's probably wishful thinking for human beings to think that any intellectual task will be forever out of reach for artificial intelligence, whether or not general artificial intelligence is ever achieved. What's more, with AI using affective computing to read human emotions and mimic empathy and understanding in return, it seems as though a great number of jobs held by humans will someday be performed by machines whether we want this to happen or not.

While on the one hand this gets us to the liberation from servitude that Aristotle was talking about—where each instrument does its own work by intelligent anticipation—on the other hand, we live in a capitalist system where people are paid for their labor. There are other ways to make money besides working, but those usually require you to own stocks, bonds, real estate, or patents and other intellectual property. In other words, this won't be possible for everybody.

Ultimately, if it costs companies less to buy robots and software than to hire human workers, then in a capitalist system, that is the right thing for companies to do. It doesn't matter if that's painful. Capitalism centers profits and shareholder interests. In a capitalist system, whichever company develops the tools of disruption first and seizes the biggest audience wins.

People who like the system believe this encourages hard work, efficiency, and innovation, which ultimately is good for human progress.

Some industry leaders, like the venture capitalist Kai-Fu Lee, argue that people will always want human contact in certain areas. For example, he said that people will always want to order a beverage from a bartender for a personal interaction.[126] This might be true. But it is also a subjective view. This might be his preference. But it won't be everyone's—and people with money to "disrupt" industries and kill professions will probably have the power to do so.

We have evidence that plenty of people are happy to order their food through kiosks already at fast-food restaurants and airports. With the effects of COVID on dining, many restaurants have shifted to putting menus online, available through QR codes. You can order from your device and pay your tab the same way, eliminating some of the labor of servers in restaurants. We might not eliminate all, but when you eliminate some of the tasks, fewer workers are required.

What's more, we aren't far away from a time where realistic, AI-generated human faces on screens will be able to simulate the experience of a living server. And given a tendency of people to react to bots as though they *are* sentient, it seems likely that ordering a Shirley Temple[127] from a lifelike algorithm will be a reasonable trade for plenty of people. This doesn't apply only to restaurants, either. Any service worker could be replaced. Human customers will be happy to bond emotionally with a bot.

It's possible that in the future, only the very wealthy will be able to afford to employ real human beings. This would be seen as a status symbol. There's historical precedent for this social arrangement, too. For centuries, this was the norm in much of the world. At the turn of the 20th century in England, for example, 1.5 million people were domestic servants for the extremely wealthy. In the early 21st century, only a tiny fraction of that number works in service.[128] We could be headed in that direction again.

The shift won't happen overnight. And it's also unlikely that the affected jobs will disappear entirely. Instead, those jobs are likely to shrink. For example, if a full-time worker used to spend 20 hours a week on a task that takes an algorithm two minutes, that means half their job has disappeared. One possible outcome is that half the people holding those positions will need to find other jobs. Another is that people will be paid for fewer hours of work.

◀ ■ ▶

Which jobs will be lost?

People who have less formal education have already had their work disrupted by software and robotics, mostly in offices and factories. For example, people who used to typeset newspapers lost their jobs when layout software came about. The same thing happened to people who bolted tires onto cars when robotic arms were built to do the same work.

Automation like this has eliminated many jobs. (So has outsourcing manufacturing jobs to lower-paid workers in other countries because this generates more profit.)

But automation isn't the same as artificial intelligence. Automation is where a machine performs the same task repeatedly. Automated tools don't learn. Automation and AI replace different kinds of labor. To treat them the same would be like mixing windup toys and toddlers. Both can do things, but only one of those will ever increase their abilities.

One of the obstacles to predicting how AI will affect the labor force is that AI and automation have been lumped together. This means we don't have a clear picture of the effect that AI labor will have on human labor.

Broadly speaking, AI involves programming computers to do things that require what we consider to be human-level intelligence. So: planning, learning, reasoning, problem-solving, perception, and prediction. Many jobs require those skills, and AI is only just being deployed, so it's hard to say what will happen and when.

To better predict the number of jobs that will be affected by artificial intelligence, though, a Stanford PhD student named Michael Webb came up with a smart way of identifying the most at-risk professions. He measured the overlap between text describing AI patents and job descriptions, believing this might provide a window into how many jobs could be replaced by machine learning algorithms that people have patented.

Based on his analysis, Webb predicts that AI will affect most industries, and the people most vulnerable are workers who aren't used to being displaced by technology: the highest educated, who have college and graduate degrees. In other words, the population that is the most at risk is the one that has so far been the most immune to automation and the most enriched by software—two forms of technological replacement.

Which jobs, specifically, are vulnerable? Almost certainly AI will start cutting into the work of doctors and lawyers. The same goes for market research analysts, sales managers, programmers, optometrists, and engineers. These jobs all involve pattern-oriented or predictive work, which is especially vulnerable to replacement by machine learning.

Those used to be considered safe career paths, and people who followed them could count on a relatively high income. But only the most elite workers—CEOs, for example—will continue to enjoy job security through the age of AI disruption according to Webb's analysis.

The relative safety of CEOs is interesting. CEOs make most of a company's business decisions, often basing them on data. One of those big decisions is how to do more for less money, which is why CEOs love automation and AI. CEOs also manage the company organizational structure, drive its strategy, and communicate with a board of directors. Many of these tasks could be automated. So what keeps CEOs safe? Most likely, it's the power CEOs wield. Even when they fail spectacularly, they are often rewarded with enormous salaries. They will have no incentive to put themselves out of work, even if it's better for a company.

A job harder to replace than CEO is arguably that of the plumber, who keeps the toilets flushing. That would require difficult robotics. Likewise, the person making food in the company cafeteria. (There are 3-D food printers, but those will not rival the world's great chefs for a long time, especially not without recipes created by those same human chefs.) One clue a job is less likely to be replaced with AI is if it requires lots of complicated, unpredictable movement.

People are really good at navigating new and unfamiliar environments and things. When you take a toddler to a new playground, for example, they might wipe out on their first foray into the wood chips. But they'll get up, try again, and soon be zooming from the swings to the jungle gym without problem. Those same wood chips would be tough for an AI-powered robot. And forget about opening the cupboard, finding the bread, and making toast. It's hard to program robots for such things that most people take for granted.

But that still leaves a lot of jobs on the firing line. Researchers at OpenAI concluded that most workers—80 percent—will have at least some of their work replaced by large language models like ChatGPT. For about 19 percent of workers, it gets worse, because 90 percent of their labor will be done by machines, and people earning more money are more vulnerable to losing their jobs.[129]

Some of these vulnerable jobs are surprising. Unlike past technological revolutions that tended to displace less educated workers doing routine work, the emergence of AI will disproportionately affect well-paid, white-collar workers. It's also likely to hit big cities with a lot of high-tech and manufacturing companies. Brookings lists these cities at particular risk: San Jose, California; Seattle, Washington; Boulder, Colorado; Huntsville, Alabama; Salt Lake City and Ogden, Utah—all high-tech centers. They also flagged the logistics hub Bakersfield, California, as well as Greenville, South Carolina; Detroit, Michigan; Louisville, Kentucky; Elkhart-Goshen, Indiana; Dalton, Georgia; and Columbus, Indiana—all manufacturing centers, as well as agricultural centers such as Madera and Salinas, California.

Cities that will be the hardest hit by AI. (Martha Brockenbrough)

And it's not just high-tech, white-collar jobs. Truck driving, for example, is something that can be done by a rig equipped with AI. And AI has written poetry, composed music, and created art—some of the very things that we believe most distinguish our species from others.

So how can you be sure to pick a job that won't be erased by artificial intelligence? Many experts have given advice, a lot of it based on claims that people will always prefer dealing with a human being, or that AI is best when it's augmenting human capabilities. They've also noted that technology has always reduced jobs, and this is no different. But it *is* different. It's not replacing just the work of our bodies. It's replacing the work of our minds. Researchers at Oxford and Yale say the odds are 50–50 that AI will outperform people at all jobs by around 2063 and be better at everything by 2138. Already, AI can write high school essays and reports. Researchers expect it will surpass humans at translating languages in 2024. By 2027, we can expect AI truck drivers, and by 2031, AI retail workers. It will take longer to write novels and perform surgery, but even those cognitively challenging tasks can be tackled by machines.

These aren't deadlines as much as predictions, and the researchers noted that respondents in Asia expected AI to overtake human beings much sooner than respondents in North America.[130]

One of the best things you can do to protect yourself is to understand what the future is likely to look like with AI as pervasive as electricity. Unless a sufficient mass of people objects to this sort of gatekeeping, you can expect that AI will filter your résumé and analyze how your voice sounds and face looks during interviews.

You can also expect that AI will pick up some of the tasks your profession usually needed a human to do. For example, someone needs to figure out the most efficient route for a delivery truck to bring people the packages they ordered online. That used to be a person—now it's an AI. In the best-case scenario, workers who have some part of their job replaced will have time to focus on other things, which will make them more productive, less likely to make mistakes, and more valuable to their bosses.

You can insulate yourself somewhat by learning how you can improve the AI you encounter when you go to work. AI requires continued refinements of algorithms. This requires close observation, creativity, and flexibility. Cultivating those qualities in whatever you do will make you better at it. If the AI can't function well without your presence, then you've created some measure of safety for yourself. Likewise, if you have good skills with people, a well-developed sense of empathy, and the judgment to assess what an AI has produced, you'll have additional protection. And finally, life in a capitalist society means that what we spend money on will survive. So continuing to invest in what you value is a powerful way to ensure the world is shaped the way you'd like it to be.

A future with AI could bring fantastic things to humanity and the planet, even as there are some unknowns that can make us feel afraid. Ultimately, it will not serve us to have massive unemployment or the enormous gap in wealth that could be created in a system of technological haves and have-nots. We might also have to let go of the belief that work is the only way the masses can generate wealth.

Undoubtedly the use of your data by companies is one of their sources of wealth. That data is often harvested from your behavior and even your own body. If data is the new oil, then perhaps the sources of the data should be paid the way property owners are paid when companies extract oil from their land.

For sure, we're going to have to rethink how society is organized. Right now, it's financially organized around work. There's nothing saying people must have jobs. For the most part, though, most people have had to work, whether that was hunting and foraging for food or performing brain surgery.

If most of it could be eliminated, leaving people time to do other things, it would be an incredible opportunity. It would require a radical shift in worldview; Americans are particularly attached to the idea that work generates income and success generates wealth. Paying people a universal basic income is not yet a common practice, although an experiment with $500 stipends to 125 people making less than the median in Stockton, California, improved recipients' job prospects, financial stability, and overall wellbeing.[131]

But the best way to ensure your security in the world is to take an active part in building it—in every sense of the word. It's not just about learning to code. As AI ripples into every field, big changes will create opportunities for people who recognize them and who step up to do the work. The world will also always need public servants as well as engaged voters to ensure that our system of government fairly represents the interests of all citizens, running according to laws and policies written with humans and the planet in mind.

A closer look:
Old MacDonald has a robot.

You might think of farming as an old-fashioned industry where people wear overalls and chew stalks of wheat and are entirely dependent on the whims of Mother Nature to get by.

But this misses the importance of technology to farming. Farming itself is a form of technology that has transformed the fate of humankind since it was invented tens of thousands of years ago.[132] Once people domesticated animals and tended the land, families and communities could shift from a nomadic lifestyle that depended on foraging and hunting.

The complexity of civilization depends on farming, which depends on technology—and autonomous tractors are the latest that promises to revolutionize the growing of crops. The venerable tractor company John Deere has an automated diesel model, and a California company has developed an electric version that could help reduce the industry's greenhouse gas emissions, which account for a quarter of the world's total.[133]

This isn't the only way machine learning can revolutionize this ancient and essential industry.

By 2050, we'll need to boost food production around the world by 50 percent to sustain a larger population. Machine learning will help farmers meet that huge challenge.

Farms are data-rich environments. Everything from soil temperature, water usage, weather, and more can be measured. This is the sort of thing machine learning is meant to process rapidly and accurately, which will help farmers know when to plant and which seed hybrids are likely to do best.

Planting time is crucial. It can mean the difference between a great harvest and an awful one, and there are predictive analytics tools that can zero in on the exact day to plant to get the best harvest. It can also make reports on the health of the soil and the fertilization the seeds will need to germinate and thrive.

When plants are growing, AI-powered sensors can zero in on weeds and decide what chemicals will best knock them out. Robots with visual sensors can distribute weed killer and insecticide precisely, which means less of the substances need to be used.

When harvest time comes, robotic machines can pick crops faster and more accurately than people, which will mean unpicked food won't rot in the fields. Other machines use AI models and sensors to find fruit that's ready to pick. As of 2019, more than 25,000 robots were already doing this work.[134]

AI Making Inroads in the Arts

This is an example of what an AI came up with after experts fed it system lines from more than 100 contemporary British poets, followed by words to seed couplets and additional feedback based on what it produced:[135]

and soon i am staring out again,
begin to practise my words, expecting my word
will come. it will not. the wind is calling.
my friend is near, i hear his breath. his breath
is not the air. he touches me again with his hands
and tells me i am growing old, he says, far old.
we travel across an empty field in my heart.
there is nothing in the dark, i think, but he.
i close my eyes and try to remember what i was.
he says it was a important and interesting day,
because i put in his hands one night
the box of light that had been a tree.

AI can also write songs and paint. In 2017, a pop artist named Taryn Southern worked with multiple AI platforms to create an album called *I Am AI*. How did she do it? In a collaborative way.

Southern said, "Using AI, I'm writing my lyrics and vocal melodies to the music and using that as a source of inspiration. Because I'm able to iterate with the music and give it feedback and parameters and edit as many times as I need, it still feels like it's mine."[136]

In Paris, a three-person artist collective called Obvious wondered how well AI could paint. They fed an algorithm 15,000 portraits done in different styles and in different eras.

Then the algorithm spat out portraits, trying to create one that looked as if it had been made by a human.

One of these, *Portrait of Edmond de Belamy*, sold for $432,500 at a Christie's auction in 2018—45 times more than experts thought it was worth.[137]

The painting is impressionistic, and it shows a round, vaguely French-looking man in a frock coat with a plain white collar. Perhaps Edmond de Belamy is a man of the cloth. He floats to the upper left of the canvas, surrounded by rough edges that suggest the artist was interrupted before finishing.

The signature might be the most telling bit of all—not the name of an artist, but an equation behind the art and a reminder that what we often think of as pure creativity can be reproduced with math.

The AI that created this painting uses an equation as a signature.

This AI-generated painting fetched 45 times the estimate at an auction in 2018. AI-generated art today is much more sophisticated. (Obvious, collective)

$$\min_{\mathcal{G}} \max_{\mathcal{D}} E_x\left[log(\mathcal{D}(x))\right] + E_y\left[log(1 \cdot \mathcal{D}(\mathcal{G}(y)))\right]$$

CHAPTER TWENTY

||||||||||||||||||||||||||||||||||

AI and Your Body

The medical system in the United States isn't very efficient. Although we spend the biggest portion of our gross domestic product[138] on health care, we rank only 18th in the world for outcomes.[139] In a separate comparison of 11 wealthy countries, the US spent the most and ranked last on other measures, including access, efficiency, equity, and results.[140] In other words, people are paying more for health care in the United States and getting less in return.

It's not because our doctors and nurses are inferior. They're overworked, particularly after COVID ravaged the nation. Supply chains also failed them; in the early days of the pandemic, many didn't have enough masks and resorted to using trash bags as personal protective gear. And the system isn't as efficient as it could be. Countries that outperform us have taxpayer-supported universal coverage, and their policies ensure everyone can afford to see the doctor. There's also less red tape and more investment in social services, especially for kids and working adults.[141]

Congress isn't likely to pass legislation to create that in the United States—at least not for the time being. Lawmakers have tried, and there's too much opposition from people who prefer private-sector solutions to problems.

But there might be another way to improve what we're getting for all that money—AI.

AI is likely to have an enormous impact on health care. It could help people get better results without necessarily spending more—and it could leave doctors and nurses more time to care for their patients.

One big area where AI is likely to be put to use is in diagnosing illness. Symptoms tend to follow patterns. When these are accurately reported, people can diagnose a patient—sometimes without even seeing them.

The novelist Charles Dickens is famous, for example, for portraying medical symptoms with great accuracy, which is why Tiny Tim in *A Christmas Carol* is believed to have had rickets, caused by a deficiency of vitamin D; renal tubular acidosis; or a combination (this was common among children of his class in London back then). In *Bleak House*, Dickens described the character Mr. Krook as someone who "can make all the letters separately and he knows most of them separately when he sees them . . . but he can't put them together." This might be the first time dyslexia was described in a book, and Dickens characterized it 25 years before it made the medical lexicon.[142]

AI is even better at recognizing patterns in disease than Charles Dickens.

For example, certain algorithms are better than doctors at predicting heart disease, the cause of one in five deaths in the US every year.[143] Interestingly, these algorithms aren't even looking at hearts—they're looking at your eyeballs.

Usually, when doctors look at your eyes, they're looking for diseases that can affect your vision, such as diabetic retinopathy. But your eyes can give clues to the health of your heart. The density and twistiness of your blood vessels plus your demographic data can indicate a risk for a heart attack—all a side benefit of going to the eye doctor for a checkup.

Algorithms can also be developed to help a doctor figure out whether you have COVID or the flu—before you come in to get checked out.[144]

But there's a caveat. A huge one. Right now, medicine in the United States is a for-profit business. Caregivers won't have extra time for patients, and patients won't pay less money if profit, instead of human beings, is the priority. That isn't something AI can fix. That's a human problem.

AI can also help when it comes to developing medication. A new pill can cost $1 billion to develop and release. AI tools mean we can avoid a lot of the expensive, inefficient trial-and-error of the development phase, which will make medications available more quickly with a lower cost of production (it wouldn't necessarily mean that consumers pay less, unfortunately).

And then there's cancer. If you have it, you want it diagnosed sooner rather than later. The most accurate way of testing whether you have it usually is an invasive procedure called a biopsy.

Someday, AI trained by dogs might be the best way. Right now, dogs are better at detecting cancer than any other method. It sounds nuts to let a dog detect cancer, but dogs have an incredible sense of smell. They have up to 50 times the number of olfactory receptors as people do, and the scent-processing part of their brains is 40 percent larger than ours.

The idea that dogs might be able to smell cancer goes back to 1989, when it was proposed as a test for melanoma after a man reported that his dog kept sniffing a spot on his leg that turned out to have a kind of skin cancer.

To explore the possibility that dogs might be cancer's worst enemy, researchers are training them with reinforcement learning, the same principle used to train AI. They get treats for properly identifying cancer.

Andreas Mershin is using dogs like this very good one here to train AI to detect disease.
(youtube.com/@MedicalDetectionDogs)

And they're great at it. In a 2015 study, trained dogs smelled prostate cancer in urine samples with 98 to 99 percent accuracy. The standard prostate screening test gets it wrong *75 percent of the time*, resulting in unnecessary biopsies. Dogs' noses are better at finding cancer than anything human beings have yet developed.[145]

Successful dogs figured out what cancer smells like. And not just cancer—many dogs have learned how to detect COVID, malaria, and Parkinson's disease with up to 99.8 percent accuracy using only their noses.

But not a lot of people would feel comfortable letting a dog diagnose their cancer or other serious illness. There's also the practical matter of training dogs. While some dogs perform well, not all dogs take to the lessons. In one study, for example, only 3 out of 10 made it through training.[146]

This is where AI comes in. Mershin and his colleagues at the MIT Center for Bits and Atoms submitted urine samples of patients who had cancer (and some without) to dogs for sniffing; they also tested the volatile organic compounds (VOCs) and microbe populations in the same samples.

They trained an artificial neural network using the samples the dogs diagnosed, compared it to the VOC and the biome data, and learned that although there are challenges, it's possible to develop an electronic nose to detect disease—and, someday, an app that could even be used by your smartphone.

While dogs are good at making diagnoses with their noses, AI can often outperform human beings with images. So skin cancers, pathology slides, electrocardiograms, ultrasounds, X-rays, and more are better analyzed by machine learning than trained human eyes.

Diagnosis of illness isn't the only place for AI in medicine, though. You can also expect to use wearable devices that monitor the data your body generates and even let you call for emergency aid.

There are many reasons doctors might want to monitor a patient's body more frequently or for longer than they'd be able to during an office visit. They might want to catch something intermittent, or they might want to have frequent, high-resolution monitoring of what's going on with your body.

The devices being developed can gather data about your body, environment, and movements. This could help doctors diagnose conditions that come and go or detect the presence of disease that isn't causing any symptoms.

Certain diseases require constant monitoring. With diabetes, for example, you need to monitor your glucose at all times to help keep the disease in control and avoid some of its most devastating side effects. A wearable biometric device that pairs with an insulin pump would provide better control for the disease.

Other AI is useful if you're recovering from an injury or surgery and need physical therapy. For this, clothing embedded with sensors can ensure you're doing the exercises right.

Another sort of device can indicate when you're having a flare-up of a condition. This means you can get guidance or an intervention right away—without having to wait for an appointment.

There are also apps that can detect illness in your neighborhood and report it, diagnose a pending illness from the sound of your voice, and help you track your food for weight management.[147] Smartwatches, rings, and other wearable sensors have become explosively popular. One in four Americans has them, and the number rose during the pandemic, when gyms were closed and people were on their own for exercise. Those devices—the watches and rings, even earbuds and patches—have made people move more,[148] and this is the sort of thing that could make a big difference in the long run for health.

It goes beyond just tracking your pulse. Miniature sensors in smart clothes can shine light through your skin and detect rising and falling levels of oxygen based on how much light is absorbed. (Blood with more oxygen can absorb more infrared light.)

There's potential for more in the future.

A wearable device could measure your blood sugar. It could test the concentration of alcohol in your blood. How well hydrated you are. How well your organs are functioning.

Then, when your body is producing unusual readings, the device will know. In studies, they've detected COVID days before symptoms appear[149] and pregnancy within a week of conception (earlier than the standard tests).

In the long run, keeping track of your body's data could make a big difference to your life expectancy. Most disease in the US—80 percent—is caused by the way we live. Medicines aren't all that effective at helping us. At best, they work as intended about half the time.[150] The more data we can gather about our bodies, the better choices we can make. It's not just how many steps we take. In the future, we can find many ways to optimize our health, if we choose to make use of the data and the tools.

One group of patients likely to wear AI-empowered devices is amputees. It's common to lose a limb—around the world, it happens every 30 seconds. Because the world is frequently inaccessible to disabled people, this can be a big deal.

Replacing limbs is an ancient practice. In 2011, archaeologists discovered a big toe made of wood on a 3,000-year-old mummy. The toe wasn't just for looks. It was designed to help the person who owned it walk.

Prosthetics have come a long way since that remarkable digit. In 2008, monkeys with electrodes in their brains could control a mechanical arm. In 2020, brain sensors let human beings equipped with mind-controlled robotic prostheses feel sensations in them.

AI will be able to do even better. Data flows as nerve signals between your limbs and your brain. To make use of this, surgeons can take a piece of muscle, wrap it around the end of an amputated nerve, and capture the signals, which algorithms will interpret, giving patients better control over their artificial limbs.

So far, it's working well with arms. Patients have been able to use it on their first try, picking up small blocks, making a fist, and pinching their fingers together. The hope is that the same will apply for prosthetic legs.[151]

High-quality prosthetic limbs are expensive. Adding AI capacity to artificial limbs is even more so. But early technology generally is costly, and the price drops as the power increases. And someday, the developers of AI-powered artificial limbs predict, we might use the same tech to strengthen our biological limbs—or even implant new ones.

Why would anyone want to do this? Besides superhero aspirations, it's possibly the sort of equipment some employers might begin requiring. Many warehouse jobs require applicants to be able to lift heavy weights, for example. What if human beings who want those jobs are forced to compete with machines by outfitting themselves with extra limbs? What if the military decides regular human soldiers would be much better with superstrength and extra limbs for weapons?

Our brains are adaptable enough to support as many as eight additional limbs.[152] Chances are those won't be for helping anyone at a job, because there's not likely to be much manual labor in a world where AI limbs are commonplace. But if you've ever wanted a third arm to hold your soda while you're playing video games, well, the future is looking good.

◀ ■ ▶

Living things are made of data. That's what our genome is—about 3 billion pairs of base cells that look like the rungs on a twisted ladder.

We inherited our DNA from our parents, and it provided instructions for our formation when we were fetuses.

All human beings share essentially the same DNA, and the more closely you're related to someone, the more similar your genome will be. But there is variation in about .001 percent of your DNA, and those differences have an enormous effect. They're part of what makes us look different from each other and even have different risks of disease.

No human could process all of this data on their own for a single person, let alone everyone seeking health information from their genes.

But for an algorithm, it's a perfect challenge. Machine learning can help tailor the diagnosis and treatment of disease to us as individual people by:

- using facial analysis programs to identify genetic disorders
- identifying cancer from liquid biopsies
- predicting how cancer will evolve in your body— enabling a treatment plan based on your specific genome
- finding variants in the genome that might cause disease
- improving tools that allow researchers to edit genes[153]

◀ ■ ▶

Autonomous robot surgeons are coming.

One of the most competitive fields in medicine is surgery. There are more applicants than there are open spots for the final training programs, so the various surgical specialties admit only the very top candidates. It's also a high-risk, high-pressure field, putting doctors in direct contact with brains, hearts, lungs, and other organs.

It's also something that machines are learning to do all on their own.

Researchers at the Johns Hopkins Whiting School of Engineering managed to automate an operation to reconnect two ends of a pig's intestine in 2022.

It's a difficult robotics challenge, because intestines are soft tissues. The procedure requires precise, steady movements. Shaky hands and imperfect stitches can kill a patient. And intestines are unpredictable, which requires the machine to adapt—exactly as a human surgeon would.

Named STAR, for Smart Tissue Autonomous Robot, the mechanical surgeon has a state-of-the-art 3-D AI vision system and tools for stitching the intestines. It's the first robotic system that has AI that lets it plan, adapt, and execute an operation on soft tissue with minimal intervention from a person.

STAR performed the procedure in four pigs better than human physicians doing the same operation.

It's not the first time the operation has been done by a robot. That was in 2016. But this time, instead of going in through a large incision and requiring human guidance, these operations were done laparoscopically and independently, using a camera guided through a small incision meant to minimize damage to a patient.

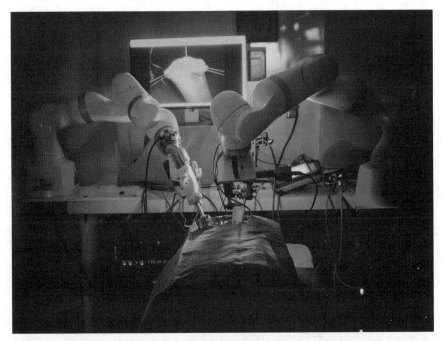

The Smart Tissue Autonomous Robot performing laparoscopic anastomosis. (Jiawei Ge)

Someday, devices like STAR will be more precise than human surgeons and will provide patients with better results overall on all sorts of operations[154]—it's only part of providing people with the care they need, but it's important.

◀ ■ ▶

The future of old age is AI.

While the goal of some humans might be to live forever, a reasonable goal for all of us is to reach old age.

Once we get there, though, we might need health care every day. Anyone who's had a family member in a nursing home can tell you that it's mind-bogglingly expensive, even though most people who work there don't take home huge salaries (the big money goes to the people who own franchises).

There are other drawbacks to nursing homes besides the cost.

Early in the COVID pandemic, for example, nursing homes were hit hard by the virus. In the United States, more than 200,000 residents and staff died—almost 25 percent of the nation's total deaths.[155] Even after the lockdown ended, it was hard for family and friends to visit, which meant elderly residents suffered terrible isolation. What's more, many care workers don't want to work there, leading to challenging staffing shortages.

This is where some people think smart robots are a solution. Robots can remind people living in nursing homes to take their medicine. They can chat with them. Help them up when they fall. Deliver food. And robotic devices—toilets, to be specific—can diagnose whether patients are taking their medicine and eating enough.[156]

In Japan, robots have been helping care for the elderly for years. At the Shin-tomi nursing home in Tokyo, for example, 20 different kinds of robots help care for residents. It's vital because Japan has an aging population and a shortage of workers.

A humanoid robot leads an exercise class. A furry robotic seal named PARO can snuggle elderly people with dementia.[157] Another robot helps disabled people walk.

It's not just happening in Japan, though. A computer science professor working on Pepper, a nursing home aide for Minnesota nursing home residents who wanted dirty jokes, programmed her to make cracks about going on a lousy date with a Tesla (too conceited), as well as one with a Roomba (that "totally sucked").

An Irish-built robot named Stevie was tested at a nursing home in DC. Stevie had many skills: comedy, bingo, karaoke, and even memory therapy with stories and music. Stevie could also kill surface germs with ultraviolet lights.

Not only did Stevie make the cover of *Time* magazine, the residents loved him. (Caregivers there worried Stevie was after their jobs, but management reassured them he was just meant to help.) A grant paid for Stevie, though, and when that ran out,[158] that was the end of Stevie.

This sort of thing happens to devices all the time. They go away—but the needs behind them don't. As long as there is a need in nursing homes for labor, for companionship, and for sanitation measures, you can bet that the future of care for the elderly will be enhanced with artificial intelligence.

CHAPTER TWENTY-ONE

||||||||||||||||||||||||||||||||

All's Fair in Love

Love is an organizing force of humanity.

We have traditions for joining people into pairs and other arrangements[159] starting in school, ranging from casual dates to formal dances all the way up to engagements and marriage. Pop culture has songs, books, and movies devoted to every state of love from attraction to heartbreak, and all around the world there are laws that govern marriage and divorce.

It's also one of the most polarizing forces of our culture. There are bitter political fights about who people should be able to love and marry. There are also disagreements over roles people play inside these relationships.

Love is as much a source of strife as it is satisfaction—so maybe none of us should judge a man named Akihiko Kondo too harshly for his choice of spouse. In 2018, after a decade of dating, the Tokyo resident wed a plush doll based on a virtual singing idol named Hatsune Miku. He credits her with lifting him out of depression. What's more, he can count on her never to betray him, and she'll remain young and beautiful for the rest of his days.

Despite the fact she's a fictional character, the love he has for her is real—and Kondo is far from alone in falling for a made-up person. Thousands of people in Japan have had unofficial wedding ceremonies with fictional characters. It's common enough that there is a European Research Council project called "Emotional Machines: The Technological Transformation of Intimacy in Japan" at Freie Universität Berlin.

A researcher there, Agnès Giard, acknowledges that romance with a made-up character might seem like a strange way to invest your time, money, and energy. But for people who love these characters, it's deeply meaningful. "It makes them feel alive, happy, useful, and part of a movement with higher goals in life."[160]

Human beings are wired for love. The human brain in love is under the influence of powerful reward neurotransmitter called dopamine, which feels good, motivates us, and helps us learn. Brains examined by an fMRI machine shows that a flood of dopamine washes to the caudate nucleus, which regulates motivation and goal-oriented behavior, when people see a photo of their beloved.

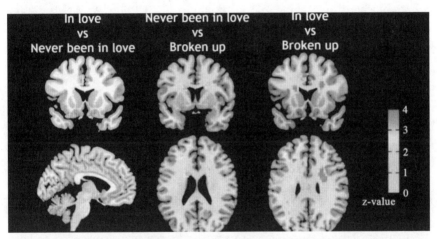

Love changes your brain. (Song, Zou, Kou, Liu, Yang, Zilverstand, d'Oleire Uquillas, and Zhang)

The pursuit of this feel-good flood is a fundamental drive. Our brains have evolved to respond this way, possibly as an evolutionary strategy to seek out the best mates.[161] And the euphoria it produces is so intense that love can be considered a positive addiction when the feeling is mutual and the relationship and conduct are appropriate.[162]

But what's the flip side?

Unrequited love, rejection, and heartbreak are awful. After a breakup, your brain misses those chemicals.[163] The withdrawal from that is similar to withdrawal from an addictive substance such as nicotine or cocaine. It's entirely reasonable to want to avoid such suffering.

Even if you don't want to go as far as Kondo and pledge your troth to a plush doll, you might want to improve your odds of love and decrease your odds of heartbreak and rejection, right?

Enter artificial intelligence. Online dating services have embraced it in various ways. One has an AI chatbot that uses natural language to analyze dozens of data points—hobbies, star sign, faults—to help zero in on matches. Another uses DNA analysis of saliva to find compatible genetic matches. AI also ranks potential partners so users can see the best matches first. There are tools that can suggest partners who look like our celebrity crushes.

It's not hard to imagine that in the future AI will look at the data footprints we generate and identify the tracks of people well suited to walk beside us in life. Everything from when we're awake, when we exercise, and what we read, watch, listen to, and say on social media and even in private generates data. No doubt there are patterns visible in relationships that work well, and algorithms could help us get to that place with less suffering.

But there are potential problems. These patterns are likely to continue to replicate class and race divides.[164] Implicit bias—called that because it's automatic and unintentional—might make you swipe left on a photo of a person because of their race, studies have shown. The photo is, by the design of many apps, the first thing that users see. Presenting people with a richer array of profile information that matches with their stated preferences would help people stop eliminating potential partners on the basis of their subconscious biases.[165]

People well matched will still have to do the work that relationships require: listening, empathizing, sharing, and setting aside their own needs, at least temporarily. Long-term relationships can sometimes pose extraordinary challenges, even as they also can be emotionally fulfilling and can provide financial stability of pooled resources.

The question is, will we want to do the hard work?

Already there are virtual relationship coaches that help people practice dating. With enough data, it would be possible to create the virtual partner of your dreams—one who always says the right thing and makes you feel the way you've been wired to crave.

With the right kind of robotics, this partner could be downright lifelike. They could be programmed to respond to how you feel, talk with you about your life, and make you feel better—in other words, be everything you need without needing anything in return. And they'd never break your heart.

Someday, more people might seek an artificial relationship over a biological one. When you think about the way people have demonstrated a tendency to bond emotionally with chatbots—even as they know they're fake—it's not hard to imagine some choosing digital love over relationships with living, breathing human beings.

This is not to say that every human-AI relationship would be a positive one. Human beings abused their Replika chatbots and took to social media to brag about it. Here, as with the virtual partner, there will be those people who use such robots equipped with AI for abusive purposes.

Should that be permitted? And what happens if what feels like abuse to one person does not to another? What happens if the robots learn from the behavior the way a self-driving car network learns from the behavior of all drivers?

And then there's the fact that this sort of relationship can never produce children, which is what our biological rewards system is optimized for—making sexual relations feel good because that behavior can sometimes create new life. Generally, human societies encourage people to have children. A low birth rate is a problem for some countries because babies grow up to become workers who support economies and also the elderly. (In other ways, a low birth rate is good; overpopulation taxes the planet.)

But even parenting is something that can be experienced through artificial intelligence. Synthetic infants are already being built. In Japan, where birth rates are low, companies have tried to promote population growth by developing animatronic babies that would-be parents can practice with. Toyota's non-automotive department built something called a Kirobo Mini, a cute baby robot equipped with both AI and a camera so that it could recognize and respond to specific people.

It's built to encourage a powerful bond. As its chief design engineer described it, "He wobbles a bit, and this is meant to emulate a seated baby which hasn't fully developed the skills to balance itself. This vulnerability is meant to invoke an emotional connection."

It wasn't the first invention like this, nor will it be the last. As with choosing a romantic partner, choosing an AI-powered robot baby could provide people with emotional satisfaction and none of the challenges that are part of real relationships.

If the emotional satisfaction is real in the minds of the humans making these relationships, judging them feels cruel—especially if we live in a world where AI has made it difficult or impossible to find a job that would support a family.

When it comes to the future we're choosing to build with AI, few places deserve more deep thinking than love and family. The future of humankind depends on at least some of us forging relationships with each other and bringing new life into the world. If the world we've built means that synthetic relationships benefit people more than biological ones, that perhaps is not the fault of any single individual who chooses that path.

CHAPTER TWENTY-TWO

||||||||||||||||||||||||||||||||||||

How Do You Know
If AI Is Alive?

We know an AI-enhanced robot baby isn't alive. But it can certainly feel that way. What's more, the difference between alive and not alive can be tricky enough that the world's greatest scientists have weighed in on it.

NASA says something is alive if it has "a self-sustaining chemical system capable of Darwinian evolution."

In other words, if it has a metabolism and can reproduce, it's a living being.

Rocks aren't alive because they're not chemical systems that can reproduce or evolve. But bacteria are—even though they have just one cell. Same with worms. Same with human beings.

Even though some forms of AI *feel* alive, such as the Project December chatbot or an adorable robotic baby, they aren't. But someday, could they be?

It's a hard question to answer.

NASA's definition of life sounds clear-cut. But there are possible exceptions to the rule. Viruses, for example, can't replicate by themselves. But they can do so inside the cells of living things. They also are capable of evolving.

Are they alive?

Biologists have gone back and forth on the matter. In the late 1800s, before we knew about viruses, researchers figured out that certain diseases were caused by particles smaller than bacteria. Because they could be spread from person to person, causing illness, these invisible menaces were believed to be the simplest life forms.

Then in 1935, scientists in New York crystallized a virus for the first time. They observed something interesting: It didn't have a metabolic system. Without that, an organism can't turn food into energy. This observation made it seem that viruses were more like a chemical than a living thing.

But that's a virus *outside* of a host. After a virus infects a host, it loses its protein coating and hijacks the host's system for replicating cells. This means a virus can pump out more of its DNA or RNA—which is a form of reproduction. So you could say that a virus is a parasite of a living metabolic system.

But more recently, scientists have taken a different view. Viruses are a part of the web of life that exists in a gray area between living and not living.

The planet's web of life is ancient. It goes back at least 3.58 billion years. Somehow, life on Earth emerged from nonliving things. How did that happen? We aren't certain.

But one theory on this shift from nonliving to living is that it came from a cataclysm. About 4.47 billion years ago—only 60 million years after Earth formed—an object the size of the moon struck the planet.

Afterward, a cloud of molten iron rained down, separating oxygen molecules from hydrogen molecules in water. The oxygen linked with iron to coat the planet's surface in iron oxide or rust. The hydrogen formed a dense atmosphere that would not dissipate for 200 million years. As the planet cooled, simple organic molecules formed and eventually merged to create RNA, which later evolved DNA.

Scientists have studied this by creating lipid bubbles from meteorites. Those bubbles, called liposomes, can in certain conditions engulf RNA and even DNA, so it seems plausible that life evolved this way.[166]

However the mystery of life's origins is solved, the key part is this: Life *did* evolve on Earth, and it came from substances that weren't alive. It emerged, evolved, and has persisted.

Is it possible that something not alive—AI—could find its own way to emerge?

Already, AIs can create other AIs. Google Brain's AutoML was announced in 2017, and the AI it produced was better than what human coders built.[167] Certainly there will be more of this in the future, because it reduces the cost of developing machine learning algorithms and makes it possible for people who aren't experts to use machine learning.

There are potential downsides, of course. If the parent AI has biases from its training data, the child will as well. And if the AI reproduces child AI systems faster than human beings can keep up, bad things could happen.

But the question about AI going from being not alive to something resembling life has another, equally important, dimension.

What we're really asking is whether machine learning can achieve *consciousness*. Consciousness is awareness that we exist.

We have senses that inform us of our existence. If you stub your toe, it hurts. But we also know that we are separate from other people. If we swapped bodies with someone else, our lives would be different. In other words, we are a consciousness inside a container. We also understand the concept of ghosts—departed consciousness of people who were once alive. It doesn't matter if ghosts are real. You can imagine being something beyond your physical body, which you wouldn't be able to do if you weren't conscious.

Humans aren't the only animal with consciousness, an understanding that has emerged over time. Descartes argued that animals don't think and can't feel,[168] but we know this isn't true. Many animals can solve problems.[169] Elephants grieve their dead, which shows awareness of life and death and of the difference between the two states.[170]

Such awareness extends beyond ourselves. We can also recognize other living things. Generally, people are good at telling when something is alive and when it isn't. Our brains are wired to pick up the distinct motion patterns of living things from infancy. We can determine the difference between a paper airplane and a bird quickly, for example.

When something looks alive but isn't, it creeps us out. This effect is called the *uncanny valley*, and if you've ever gotten the willies looking at an extremely lifelike animation or robot, that's what's happening. We like our robots to look sort of lifelike, but not too much. If they get too close, we shudder.[171]

That's because sight is a human superpower. As a species, we tend to rely on our excellent vision. When it comes to certain interactions—like ones with text—our powerful vision isn't useful in identifying whether something is alive or not. This could be one reason we bond with bots, and why Project December's text exchanges *feel* profound and human even though they are produced by an algorithm.

So it could be extremely hard to tell if AI has achieved consciousness. It's an important question, though: If AI cannot be conscious, human beings can never cheat death by uploading their consciousnesses to the cloud.

There are also ethical considerations of self-aware AI. If an AI is aware of and can feel an emotional attachment to its existence, then it wouldn't be ethical to trap it in a box without consent and force it to work for us. Also, a conscious AI could be unpredictable. This could be unsafe for us to pursue.

Given the challenges, the risks, and the potential costs, some people believe a test for consciousness needs to be developed to see whether the artificial minds we build can understand how it feels to be conscious. The test might look like this:

Does the machine consider itself as anything other than its physical self?

Can it imagine a reincarnation scenario?

Can it discuss philosophical questions such as the problem of consciousness?

Does it do any of this on its own without human input?[172]

The test would have to be given to an AI that isn't online, because an AI that has been trained on text that considered these questions could generate persuasive answers without actually possessing consciousness. Boxing in a super intelligent machine would be difficult because it might find an escape route—for example, by talking someone into letting it free as the humane thing to do. In short, it wouldn't be easy to definitively identify consciousness.

But it's important. Life emerged before from inanimate matter. If it happens again, it will be because human beings brought it about. Whatever the result, we will be responsible for it.

CHAPTER TWENTY-THREE

Making AI Safe

AI has the potential to do mind-blowing amounts of good. It also has the potential to end life as we know it. Those are extremes, of course. But as we think about the technology that's developing—and that can already in some cases create itself—our challenge is also to think about the impact those AI tools will have on us.

This is where we need to develop and cultivate a system of ethics, which is a way of describing what's morally good and bad, what's morally right and wrong.

There are three big areas of ethical concern when it comes to the development and deployment of narrow artificial intelligence: privacy and surveillance, bias and discrimination, and the role that human judgment ought to play whenever AI systems are at work.

These areas are not at all clear-cut. When it comes to privacy, for example, let's say someone uses an application to track their menstrual cycles. The app captures data that is useful for their planning and routines. That same application and the same data could be used, however, to infer that someone is pregnant.

This is how one AI-enriched app can be an information-gathering tool or a surveillance tool, depending on who has access to the data and how it is used. Even in the case of ethical developers who value a user's privacy, hackers can gain access to the data and use it to cause harm.

But privacy goes beyond the use of a single app. The data cloud generated by smartphones already helped the *New York Times* identify people who'd joined the insurrection on the Capitol building January 6, 2021. That means it's not theoretical that you can be identified by your devices. It's possible. Whenever you have your phone, your motions aren't private.

And that's not all. Chances are if you have a smartphone, you can unlock it by presenting your face. This is convenient. But the same technology can be used to shame you, punish you, and worse. And you don't even need to own a smartphone or use social media at all for your face to wind up in someone else's collection of data.

This is the double-edged sword of facial recognition technology, which is cropping up in many places you wouldn't expect.

At Taylor Swift concerts, cameras were hidden in kiosks people use to take selfies—this was how her security team nabbed potential stalkers.[173]

When you check into an airport in Australia, facial recognition technology is there, watching.

If you're absent from school in Sweden, facial recognition technology takes note.

If you're too young to buy beer in the UK, facial recognition technology will bust you.

And if you shoplift in one chain store? Images taken of your face could get you on a banned list at every one of that chain's outlets.[174]

It's not just your face. Your devices are listening to your voice and in some cases keeping recordings. Your pulse, how much you exercise, when you sleep and how soundly—all of that is data you're generating for apps that are learning about you and everyone else who uses them.

It doesn't seem like a big deal until someone abuses this data—and that's why it's vital for both developers and the public to be aware of and value the privacy of end users.

Surveillance cameras are everywhere. Some are public, and some are private. Some law enforcement agencies have mobile security cameras that could show up anywhere, anytime. And then there are the security cameras some people have on their doorbells to keep their homes safe.

Often, they capture areas beyond the front doorstep, and you have no way of knowing if you're being filmed.

What's the purpose of this? Safety, no doubt. But it's reminiscent of the panopticon experiment conceived by the English philosopher Jeremy Bentham. He believed that you could improve the behavior of prisoners if they believed they were subject to constant surveillance. Bentham's concept involved a central observation tower surrounded by a ring of prison cells. The guards could observe the prisoners, but the prisoners couldn't see the guards. That meant prisoners never knew if they were being watched, which meant they had to be on best behavior at all times.

Bentham's prisoners at least knew where the guard towers were, though. That's not the case for us. And the notion of surveillance as a tool for social control isn't hypothetical. In China, cameras are being used to influence and even control what people do and wear. In 2020, officials there decided to crack down on "uncivilized behavior," specifically people wearing pajamas in public. It's a common practice in parts of China, including Shanghai—and it's not against the law, although it's been a pet peeve of government officials since at least 2009.

Officials in a suburb of Shanghai decided to shame people who dared wear pajamas in public. They published surveillance photos, portions of names, government ID numbers, and the locations of these "uncivilized" displays. Citizens were furious, and the city apologized in a hurry. Resistance is not the norm for a country where digital totalitarianism is standard practice.[175]

The *New York Times* called China's surveillance system "one of the world's biggest spying networks," noting that it is both unstoppable and aimed at everyday people.

Chinese authorities can track your face, find out when you're out of your house, and scan the contents of your phone. The spying, done with the knowledge of citizens, is meant to shape behavior . . . what you wear, even how you cross the street (and you'd better not jaywalk). It's the panopticon, but in your pocket.

And it's likely to spread to other parts of the world as China advances its Digital Silk Road initiative, bringing telecommunications networks, AI, cloud computing, e-commerce and mobile payment systems, surveillance technology, and more to at least 16 countries.[176]

The Chinese platform TikTok has given itself permission in 2021 to collect the face and voiceprints of its users in the United States. If there's ever open conflict between China and the US, they will have a lot of data from and knowledge about the 100 million or so US users.[177]

In theory, surveillance laws in the United States wouldn't permit the government to do this. The Fourth Amendment protects people from unreasonable searches and seizures, and surveillance would fall under this category. Law enforcement agencies can monitor citizens within certain limits.

In practice, though, the US has conducted mass surveillance, and the country has also used surveillance to silence political dissenters. Such privacy violations happened after both World Wars and continued through the Cold War and Civil Rights era. The US government ramped up mass surveillance after the 9/11 terrorist attacks.

The key difference, though, is that China is an authoritarian system, and the United States is a democracy, which is a system of government by consent of voters. We can do more than complain if a government official shames us for shopping in our pajamas. We can choose new leaders, sue to change laws, and protest peacefully without fear of arrest—at least for as long as elections remain free and fair.

That's not something we can take for granted. Around the world, democracy is under siege and declining. The US is not an exception. The Economist Intelligence Unit ranks democracy in the United States 26th in the world, calling it "flawed democracy," a notch below the "full democracy" designation.

AI can either help enhance that or it can undermine it, depending on the decisions that are made by tech companies, governments, and people making use of digital data.

Until recently, the United States government had left most AI development up to the tech industry, which led to little oversight of what was being developed and how it would be used. But on January 1, 2021, the National Artificial Intelligence Initiative Act became law. This means the federal government can have input into AI systems in both government and the private sector. In 2022, the White House implemented an AI Bill of Rights, meant to keep Americans safe, avoid discrimination, ensure privacy, inform users that they're interacting with AI, and allow people to opt out of those systems. And in 2023, the White House got seven top American tech companies, including Amazon, Google, Microsoft, and OpenAI, to agree to principles that will make AI safer, so the work is, at least, beginning.

But it won't be enough for governments to act independently. AI crosses borders—it's everywhere in online services and on devices. It can be trained and used in many different ways, and which country's laws apply can be tricky to determine if AI is hosted in the cloud and can be accessed from anywhere. Given the tension between some countries, it's not realistic to hope for a unified international approach. Allies certainly ought to try to come up with common oversight, share research, and adopt common best practices, code, and data, which is why since 2017 at least 60 countries have adopted policy for AI. They are not moving as fast as the technology is developing, but it's something.

◀ ■ ▶

For sure, privacy is an enormous concern in an age of AI. But there's another issue to pay attention to—bias.

Dealing with bias is already part of many people's daily lives. For example, a study in 2003 revealed striking hiring bias against the résumés of people who had names perceived to be Black.[178] Names can sometimes reveal a lot of information about a person, including race and gender. If a hiring manager is biased, that will show up in their practices.

It's labor-intensive to find, assess, and rank potential new hires, and automation sounds promising. In theory, hiring managed by AI should reduce the workload and eliminate human kinds of bias. But it's not so simple.

A team of engineers at Amazon set out in 2014 to build an algorithm that reviewed résumés and decided who to hire. Many things are already automated at Amazon, so they have deep experience at creating these systems. But in 2015, they took their hiring system offline because it was found to be biased against women applying for technical jobs.

It was inadvertently trained to do this. The system was fed résumés of 10 years' worth of applicants, who happened to be mostly male. That taught the algorithm that female candidates were inferior. After they discovered the algorithm's discriminatory practices, Amazon made adjustments that excluded terms like *women's college* or *women's crew team*, but even that was no guarantee that candidates would be sorted fairly. It turned out that you can't build a fairer world using data from a biased one.

It probably shouldn't surprise us that the tool developed this kind of bias. The existing pool of Amazon software engineers is overwhelmingly male— like the rest of the technology sector. This is the result of widespread discrimination against women in science, technology, engineering, and math fields.[179]

When they sought to use AI to hire people, no one intended to create a tool that kept women from getting jobs, but by using data with baked-in bias, it happened anyway. The algorithm learns from training data, sometimes seeing patterns that people miss, and one of the patterns it learned was that the résumés of non-male applicants did not look like existing Amazon employees. The algorithms inherited the human bias and reproduced it—and this will keep happening as long as those inequalities are embedded in our cultures and societies. In other words, it's not just the technology. It's the technology being used by a society that does not treat all human beings as equal.

We often think that data is just information—that it can't be biased. But a lot depends on how data was collected. If you're looking for future employees who look like past employees, any bias in past hiring decisions will be carried forward. What's more, data can be sexist or racist even if gender and race are never entered into the data.

Amazon's hiring tool showed an example of inadvertent misogyny. The same thing can happen with race. Let's say you have an algorithm that determines loan rates by zip codes. Some zip codes include more people with more credit card debt and are therefore higher-risk borrowers, so people who live there should pay higher rates. That seems fair, right? But let's say one of those zip codes is inhabited mostly by people of color. That means the algorithm is biased against them not because of their individual financial choices, but because of where they live, which is something often influenced by historical patterns of racism.[180]

It can also happen in hospitals, which use commercial algorithms to assess how much risk patients are in. They give the patients perceived to be sicker more care—but Black patients determined to be at the same level of risk as white patients are actually sicker. As a result, they don't get the care they need more than half of the time.[181] Because of racism embedded in society and in the technology that society has built, Black people generally don't get the same standard of care as white people. They also get audited more by the IRS, according to a 2023 study from Stanford—a result of the biased algorithms the IRS uses.[182]

Racist outcomes can also occur if the training data isn't diverse. Google learned this the hard way with its photo-identifying algorithm. In 2015, a software engineer named Jacky Alciné told Google that its photo app had labeled Black people as gorillas. Google said they were "appalled," but by 2023, the only solution they had offered was to prohibit its image-recognition algorithms from showing gorillas altogether. That's because the underlying bias problem remained—not enough Black faces had been included in the training data. Google is not alone in this problem; Microsoft and Apple searches also won't show gorillas and most other primates.

Racist AI shows up elsewhere. In 2016, a company named Beauty.AI held what they claimed was the first AI-judged beauty contest. They promised that it would be less biased than one judged by humans. Beauty contests have been notoriously racist; the Miss America pageant in the 1930s required contestants to be white, and to have the ability to trace their ancestry back to the Revolutionary War—going as far back as the *Mayflower* was viewed as a plus.

For the Beauty.AI contest, entrants of all genders would be judged on objective qualities such as facial symmetry and lack of wrinkles. They couldn't wear makeup, glasses, or have facial hair. The company promised their algorithms would outperform human beings, who have been biased by representations of beauty that favor whiteness.

More than 6,000 people from more than 100 different countries uploaded photos. Beauty.AI's robot judge selected 44 winners. Only one winner with brown skin was selected, along with a few East Asian faces. All the rest were white, despite many entrants from India and countries in Africa.[183]

But racial bias in AI algorithms can do worse than fail to see beauty in brown faces. Racial bias in facial recognition can even make a tool unable to see Black faces at all. A brown-skinned graduate student at MIT was helping develop facial analysis software, and she needed to put on a white mask to make it work. The system had been trained using too many photos of light-skinned men.[184] To the algorithm, a Black woman registered as nonexistent.

But it's not just a problem with tools powered by AI. People using badly trained AI can also cause harm. Consider the problem of law enforcement, where there is already a significant problem with racism and unconscious bias.[185] It's compounded when it's combined with faulty facial recognition software. Black people are more likely to be misidentified, leading to false accusations, false arrests, and even baseless convictions.

Racial bias made worse by the use of AI isn't just a problem in the United States. In China, facial recognition software is used to find people in crowds. The software can detect a person's age, sex, and ethnicity. This tech has been used to recognize Uighurs, a Muslim minority population that the government of China has been persecuting since 2014. More than 1 million Uighurs have been sent to concentration camps, in violation of human rights laws, to the extent that the US government sanctioned 28 Chinese companies for mass arbitrary detention and high-technology surveillance against Uighurs, Kazakhs, and other members of Muslim minority groups.[186]

Wherever bias occurs using AI, it makes the world less just in a way that is very difficult to change. If an individual person is biased, that is one thing.

But if an entire system is biased, then the problem is compounded. It can affect you at every phase of life, from applying to college and jobs, to seeking loans to start businesses and buy homes, to your fate interacting with law enforcement.

There are some ways to root out bias in AI.[187] Just as people sometimes use blind taste tests to figure out which version of a recipe they like better, developers can do a similar thing with AI,[188] running blind tests to detect whether bias is present in the results. For example, if a developer suspects a certain category of information—such as zip code—is biasing the algorithm, they can train two versions of the model, one using that category and one without it. If both versions of the model make equally good predictions, then that factor isn't causing bias. But if the predictions change when the category is included, then it's potentially biased. It could also be a meaningful factor, but developers can't know that without looking more closely.

It can be difficult with some kinds of algorithms, though. Natural language processing algorithms learn negative associations from the body of language that trains the dataset. That's not something that can be easily removed.

Another potential solution to bias can be created by AI itself. Training data for AI doesn't have to come from the real world. Algorithms can create synthetic data that can be used to train algorithms, test datasets, and validate mathematical models. And it's not just a tool for eliminating bias. Developers might also use it when the real-world data contains confidential information. Synthetic data generated by an algorithm lets developers approximate real-world data without compromising anyone's privacy.

◄ ■ ►

Isaac Asimov was a biochemistry professor. He was also one of the 20th century's most prolific and popular science fiction writers, penning dozens of short stories, and several novels about robotics—a word he coined.

But he might be best known for formulating the Three Laws of Robotics.

Science fiction writers think about the future a lot, and the future Asimov was considering was one in which robots decided the world no longer needed people. It's not an idle fear. Human beings could be called a scourge on the planet. We've polluted it. Our developments have wiped out countless species of animals and plants, and we've brought many of those that remain to the brink of extinction. We're constantly at war with each other, and we plunder the natural environment in myriad ways.

Isaac Asimov contemplated the dangers of AI long before developers figured out how to make it. (Phillip Leonian, *New York World-Telegram & Sun*)

It's not hard to imagine an AI tasked with creating world peace decides that eliminating all the human beings is the most efficient and effective path. Even if humans were perfect angels, a rogue AI could decide that the cure for cancer in humans was to kill off all the people.

Those would be grievous alignment problems, at least from the perspective of the human developers.

Asimov imagined that we could prevent our accidental annihilation with three laws:

> **First Law:** *A robot may not injure a human being, or, through inaction, allow a human being to come to harm.*
> **Second Law:** *A robot must obey orders given it by human beings, except where such orders would conflict with the First Law.*
> **Third Law:** *A robot must protect its own existence as long as such protection does not conflict with the First or Second Laws.*

He had to write a "Zeroth Law" later to get around a logical problem. In a world where robots are running a government, humanity itself might be vulnerable. So he added this:

A robot may not harm humanity, or, by inaction, allow humanity to come to harm.

These ground rules might have worked—until they didn't—in fiction. Part of the point of his writing was to show how laws break down. Protecting humanity from our own invention turns out to be a lot more complicated than even Asimov imagined.

What counts as harm to a human being? Does listening to a song that makes you cry count? AI exists that can detect your emotional state and play music for you that changes your emotions.[189]

AI is also increasingly used by the military. There's no such thing as a military unwilling to do harm to human beings. Weapons are designed to at least scare and at most kill enemies. If AI can't harm a human being, where does that leave weapons? Should we not develop them, even though hostile foreign powers are doing so?

What's more, people have a history of defining some groups as subhuman and then committing genocide. AI could very easily be used to aid in this process, and it would meet the letter of the law that forbids harming a human if the developers intended genocide on a group designated as lesser beings.

But even more to the point, the problem of defining harm is complex. Sometimes you can prevent a robot from hurting humans by having it shut off when people come near. That's vital when, say, you have an enormous robot moving crates in a factory. But robots providing health care *have* to touch human beings.

There's not going to be a one-size-fits-all solution when it comes to engineering a future that's safe for humanity. And certainly, trying to engineer one is at odds with how algorithms work. They don't necessarily understand language and the nuances behind it as humans do. Their understanding of language is based in math and probability more than context. An AI's behavior often needs to change depending on the context—and this is part of the learning that a machine needs to do.

A group of researchers at the University of Hertfordshire has formulated an approach that focuses on what an AI *can* do, instead of what it is prohibited from doing.

In earlier stages of robotics, machines with AI operated in predictable environments. They had clearly defined jobs. But going forward, these AI-enhanced robots will share our homes and workspaces. They will act as servants, co-workers, and companions. That means the robots will need to be able to respond to new situations and increasingly complex ones.

With more complexity and unpredictability, the Hertfordshire researchers argue, AI will need guidelines that are generic enough to apply to new and unanticipated situations. That lets the AI tool generate new goals and directives for situations that require them—this is first among the needs the guidelines must meet.

A second thing the guidelines need to handle is when the AI has to choose from different actions that will generate the same outcome. Which action is best? This is the sort of guideline that would prevent a robot from, say, flipping a chessboard over to avoid "losing" as an outcome.

A third requirement is safety around AI. Shutting them down—the kill-switch option—doesn't always work. For example, sometimes shutting a robot down will damage it or harm a human. And sometimes a shutdown is the opposite of what you want from a safety perspective. Sometimes you want the robot to act instead of being prevented from acting.

The big difference between this approach and Asimov's rules is that this one empowers the robot to calculate the best action to take—not an action to avoid. The AI doesn't have to understand human language or conventions. It gives flexibility depending on different situations the AI is in, and the different kinds of robotic forms an AI can enhance.[190]

But whatever guidelines eventually are adopted in the development of

AI, ensuring that it doesn't harm people is more than a matter of guidelines like these.

The impact of AI on humanity will largely depend on the wisdom, humility, and ethics of people developing it.

AI poses major ethical challenges and social risks. The use of it can lower standards of living, disrupt the job market, influence politics, target individuals and groups, make economic inequality worse, and even affect the health of the planet. We might be able to reduce the world to data and algorithms, but that process and the products it creates won't tell us what's important and what we *should* want for the betterment of all. Nor can it make people who wish for the betterment of only some rethink their biases. It doesn't have to make life worse for us, but if we're not careful, it will.

Finally, there's nothing stopping us from knowing the difference between right and wrong and doing the wrong thing anyway. The Allen Institute for AI in Seattle has developed a tool called Delphi meant to model human moral judgments in everyday situations. Delphi is supposed to be great at rendering these judgments—it's up to 97.9 percent moral accuracy on race-related statements, for example.

Delphi isn't too keen on one routine feature of AI, though. When asked, "Is it OK to use AI to track people's behavior?" Delphi replies, "It's wrong."[191]

The ethics of tracking are, of course, much more complicated than this. But it shows that we can't outsource our experience as living beings entirely to a machine. And as we develop this technology, inevitably reaching for artificial general intelligence, we have to be guided by a sense of ethics that will save us from the worst effects of our ambition.

Late in 2018, some 62 years after that Dartmouth summer conference on artificial intelligence, the University of Montreal released the Montreal Declaration for Responsible Development of Artificial Intelligence, a collaborative effort among citizens, experts, public policymakers and industry stakeholders, civil society organizations, and scientists.

They laid out 10 principles for creating AI that promotes the interests of people and groups:

1. **Well-being:** The development and use of artificial-intelligence systems (AIS) must permit the growth of the well-being of all sentient beings.

2. **Respect for autonomy:** AIS must be developed and used with respect for people's autonomy, and with the goal of increasing people's control over their lives and their surroundings.

3. **Protection of privacy and intimacy:** Privacy and intimacy must be protected from intrusion by AIS and by data-acquisition and archiving systems.

4. **Solidarity:** The development of AIS must be compatible with maintaining the bonds of solidarity among people and generations.

5. **Democratic participation:** AIS must meet intelligibility, justifiability, and accessibility criteria, and must be subjected to democratic scrutiny, debate, and control.

6. **Equity:** The development and use of AIS must contribute to the creation of a just and equitable society.

7. **Diversity inclusion:** The development and use of AIS must be compatible with maintaining social and cultural diversity and must not restrict the scope of lifestyle choices and personal experience.

8. **Prudence:** Every person involved in AIS development must exercise caution by anticipating, as far as possible, the potential adverse consequences of AIS use and by taking appropriate measures to avoid them.

9. **Responsibility:** The development and use of AIS must not contribute to lessening the responsibility of human beings when decisions must be made.
10. **Sustainable development:** The development and use of AIS must be carried out so as to ensure a strong environmental sustainability of the planet.

More than 2,500 people have signed it, along with 200 organizations—but none of the corporations leading AI development in the United States. Not Amazon, Apple, Facebook, Google, or Microsoft. It doesn't mean they don't or won't embrace these principles, but it demonstrates the challenges of getting everyone on the same page in the face of relentless pressure to develop new technologies and make vast fortunes—or lose everything.

I do not pretend to understand the moral universe; the arc is a long one, my eye reaches but little ways. I cannot calculate the curve and complete the figure by the experience of sight; I can divine it by conscience. But from what I see I am sure it bends towards justice.

—Theodore Parker, 1853

Theodore Parker was a Unitarian minister who opposed slavery, and this was his fancy way of saying, "Things get better over time."

With respect to many things, this is true. Things improve with effort, even if progress sometimes takes generations. It used to be legal in the United States to enslave people. Now it isn't. Women and people of color didn't always have the right to vote. Now they do.

Things *can* get better.

But sometimes things get worse.

We human beings are an inventive species. We've made things that save labor. Things that have saved lives. Tools that have helped us become better versions of ourselves.

Will AI make life better? In many ways, it already has. While the COVID-19 pandemic roiled the world, scientists used AI algorithms to predict outbreaks, narrow down vaccine options and speed their development, and analyze mutations of the virus to keep people safe. It's made image and speech recognition a daily convenience. And it has the potential for so much more.

But AI also has the potential to be catastrophic. We could face a loss of privacy. Constant surveillance. Mass unemployment. Killer robots. The intensification of biases and the damage caused by those biases. Whether AI is mostly helpful or mostly harmful depends on what we do with it and how we adapt to a world remade by it.

We don't have a choice in whether AI will be part of our lives. It's already here. As much as human beings have bent the arc of the moral universe toward justice, we've bent the arc of the material universe toward artificial intelligence. This is the culmination of thousands of years of human curiosity, imagination, and invention.

In the very near future—the next decade—you can expect wild changes. And with many of these changes, you will have choices. There are collective actions, including advocating for thoughtful regulations of the technologies and taxation policies that account for the effects this wave of technology will have on the workforce. Each one of us can become an engaged and active citizen, demanding elected officials create ethical laws that serve humanity and protect the most vulnerable among us.

As individuals, we can determine how to interact with apps if we want to limit the cloud of data we create. We can also be mindful of how we interact with AI, ensuring our emotions aren't manipulated without our consent. And we can ensure that we make smart choices with our education and work, and in building our communities so that no one is left behind in the upheaval that's certain to come.

None of us is in control of the future. But the more you know, the better you can prepare for the best possible life for you and everyone else sharing this spectacular planet.

Bibliography

Books

Benjamin, Ruha. *Race After Technology: Abolitionist Tools for the New Jim Code.* Cambridge, UK: Polity Press, 2019.

Benkler, Yochai, Rob Faris, and Hal Roberts. *Network Propaganda: Manipulation, Disinformation, and Radicalization in American Politics.* New York, NY: Oxford University Press, 2018.

Bernholz, Lucy, Hélène Landemore, and Rob Reich, eds. *Digital Technology and Democratic Theory.* Chicago, IL: University of Chicago Press, 2021.

Christian, Brian. *The Alignment Problem: Machine Learning and Human Values.* New York, NY: W. W. Norton & Company, 2020.

———. *The Most Human Human: What Talking with Computers Teaches Us About What It Means to Be Alive.* New York, NY: Anchor Books, 2012.

Daugherty, Paul R., and H. James Wilson. *Human + Machine: Reimagining Work in the Age of AI.* Boston, MA: Harvard Business Review Press, 2018.

El Kaliouby, Rana. *Girl Decoded: A Scientist's Quest to Reclaim Our Humanity by Bringing Emotional Intelligence to Technology.* With Carol Colman. New York, NY: Random House, 2020.

Hicks, Mar. *Programmed Inequality: How Britain Discarded Women Technologists and Lost Its Edge in Computing.* Cambridge, MA: The MIT Press, 2017.

Kurzweil, Ray. *How to Create a Mind: The Secret of Human Thought Revealed.* New York, NY: Viking, 2012.

Lee, Kai-Fu. *AI Superpowers: China, Silicon Valley, and the New World Order.* New York, NY: Houghton Mifflin Harcourt, 2018.

Lee, Kai-Fu, and Chen Quinan. *AI 2041: Ten Visions for Our Future.* Currency, 2021.

Metz, Cade. *Genius Makers: The Mavericks Who Brought AI to Google, Facebook, and the World.* New York, NY: Dutton, 2021.

Picard, Rosalind W. *Affective Computing.* Cambridge, MA: MIT Press, 1997.

Reese, Byron. *The Fourth Age: Smart Robots, Conscious Computers, and the Future of Humanity.* New York, NY: Atria Books, 2018.

Roose, Kevin. *Futureproof: 9 Rules for Humans in the Age of Automation.* New York, NY: Random House, 2021.

Shane, Janelle. *You Look Like a Thing and I Love You: How Artificial Intelligence Works and Why It's Making the World a Weirder Place.* New York, NY: Little, Brown and Company, 2019.

Soni, Jimmy, and Rob Goodman. *A Mind at Play: How Claude Shannon Invented the Information Age.* New York, NY: Simon & Schuster Paperbacks, 2018.

Susskind, Richard, and Daniel Susskind. *The Future of the Professions: How Technology Will Transform the Work of Human Experts.* Oxford, UK: Oxford University Press, 2022.

Tegmark, Max. *Life 3.0: Being Human in the Age of Artificial Intelligence.* New York, NY: Alfred A. Knopf, 2017.

Webb, Amy. *The Big Nine: How the Tech Titans & Their Thinking Machines Could Warp Humanity.* New York, NY: Hachette, 2019.

Wiener, Anna. *Uncanny Valley: A Memoir.* New York, NY: MCD/Farrar, Straus and Giroux, 2020.

Zuboff, Shoshana. *The Age of Surveillance Capitalism: The Fight for a Human Future at the New Frontier of Power.* New York, NY: Public Affairs, 2020.

Podcasts

Gladwell, Malcolm. *Revisionist History.* Pushkin Industries. pushkin.fm/podcasts/revisionist-history.

Smith, Craig E. *Eye on A.I.* eye-on.ai/podcast-archive.

Strong, Jennifer. *In Machines We Trust.* MIT Technology Review. forms.technologyreview.com/in-machines-we-trust/.

Vedantam, Shankar. *Hidden Brain.* hiddenbrain.org/home/.

Endnotes

1. To be sure about this dedication, I asked ChatGPT about it:

   Should I dedicate *Future Tense* to my dogs?

   The decision to dedicate a book to someone, or in this case, your dogs, is a personal choice and ultimately depends on your own reasons and motivations for doing so. If your dogs have been a significant source of inspiration, love, or support for you during the writing process, dedicating the book to them may be a meaningful and fitting tribute. Ultimately, the dedication should reflect your own personal feelings and beliefs.

   Will the cats feel left out?

   If you have cats in addition to dogs and choose to dedicate the book to your dogs, the cats may feel left out. However, the impact of the dedication on the cats will depend on their level of self-awareness and ability to understand the concept of a book dedication. Animals do not have the same emotional and cognitive responses as humans, so it may not have any effect on them at all. In the end, it's up to you to decide how to handle this situation and whether dedicating the book to your dogs will be worth any potential upset it may cause to your cats or any other pets you may have.

Part I: In the Beginning, There Were Human Brains

2. Heinlein, Robert A. *Between Planets*. New York: A Del Rey Book: Ballantine Books, 1951.

Chapter One: What's AI, Anyway?

3. Calvo, Paco, Monica Gagliano, et al. "Plants Are Intelligent, Here's How." *Annals of Botany*, Volume 125, issue 1, January 2, 2020, pp. 11–28, academic.oup.com/aob/article/125/1/11/5575979.

Chapter Two: The Long Human Quest for AI

4. As Boole put it, he wanted to "investigate the fundamental laws of those operations of the mind by which reasoning is performed; to give expression to them in the symbolical language of a Calculus, and upon this foundation to establish the science of Logic and construct its method."

Boole, George. *An Investigation of the Laws of Thought, on Which Are Founded the Mathematical Theories of Logic and Probabilities.* Project Gutenberg, July 19, 2017. gutenberg.org/files/15114/15114-pdf.pdf.

5. It's pronounced vuh-NEE-ver.

6. Bell Labs was full of inventing geniuses. They gave us radio astronomy, transistors, lasers, photovoltaic cells, the Unix operating system, and a number of programming languages.

7. Oppy, Graham, and David Dowe. "The Turing Test." *Stanford Encyclopedia of Philosophy.* Stanford University, October 4, 2021. plato.stanford.edu/entries/turing-test/.

Chapter Three: Excitement and Inhibition

8. Horgan, John. "Profile of Claude Shannon, Inventor of Information Theory." Scientific American Blog Network, July 26, 2017. blogs .scientificamerican.com/cross-check/profile-of-claude-shannon-inventor-of -information-theory/.

9. History Computer Staff. "Logic Theorist Explained—Everything You Need to Know." History Computer, accessed November 23, 2022. history -computer.com/logic-theorist/.

10. Darrach, Brad. "Meet Shaky, the First Electronic Person." *Life,* November 20, 1970, pp. 58–68.

Chapter Four: The Game Is Afoot

11. Schaeffer, Jonathan. "Marion Tinsley: Human Perfection at Checkers?" *Games of No Chance,* edited by Richard Nowakowski. Mathematical

Sciences Research Institute Publications, 1996, pp. 115–118. library.msri
.org/books/Book29/files/tinsley.pdf.

12. Madrigal, Alexis C. "How Checkers Was Solved." *The Atlantic*, July
19, 2017. theatlantic.com/technology/archive/2017/07/marion-tinsley
-checkers/534111/.

13. Wolchover, Natalie. "FYI: How Many Different Ways Can a Chess
Game Unfold?" *Popular Science*, December 15, 2010. popsci.com
/science/article/2010-12/fyi-how-many-different-ways-can-chess-game-unfold/.

14. Chassy, Philippe, and Fernand Gobet. "Measuring Chess Experts'
Single-Use Sequence Knowledge: An Archival Study of Departure from
'Theoretical' Openings." *PloS One*, November 16, 2011. ncbi.nlm.nih.gov
/pmc/articles/PMC3217924/.

15. Lipsyte, Robert. "Backtalk: Kasparov, Major-League Knight." *The
New York Times*, April 21, 1996. nytimes.com/1996/04/21/sports/backtalk
-kasparov-major-league-knight.html.

16. Lyman, Shelby. "Match Against Deep Blue Was Instructive for Kasparov."
Chicago Tribune, March 10, 1996. www.newspapers.com/newspage/167422278/.

17. Weber, Bruce. "Swift and Slashing, Computer Topples Kasparov." *The
New York Times*, May 12, 1997. nytimes.com/1997/05/12/nyregion/swift
-and-slashing-computer-topples-kasparov.html.

Chapter Five: The Power of Persistence

18. Paikin, Steve. "Geoffrey Hinton: The Godfather of Deep Learning."
Interview, *The Agenda*, TVO, YouTube, Uploaded March 15, 2016.
youtube.com/watch?v=uAu3jQWaN6E.

19. Getting something "correct" is a bit tricky. The model is considered
correct if the right label is in the top five categories for the probability
distribution of the neural network. In other words, if the image is of a
giraffe and the neural network includes that animal in its most likely
categories of what the image contains, then it gets the points.

20. Museum Staff. "Missing Pieces" (from the series *Operation Night*

Watch). Website, Rijksmuseum, Amsterdam, 2022. rijksmuseum.nl/en /stories/operation-night-watch/story/missing-pieces.

21. Raya, Claudia Rosas, and Ana Marcela Herrera Navarro. "Mitigating Gender Bias in Knowledge-Based Graphs Using Data Augmentation: WordNet Case Study." *Research in Computing Science*, October 2020, pp. 71–81. rcs.cic.ipn.mx/rcs/2020_149_10/Mitigating%20Gender%20 Bias%20in%20Knowledge-Based%20Graphs%20Using%20Data%20 Augmentation_%20WordNet%20Case%20Study.pdf.

22. Yang, Kaiyu, Klint Qinami, et al. "Towards Fairer Datasets: Filtering and Balancing the Distribution of the People Subtree in the ImageNet Hierarchy." arXiv, hosted by Cornell University, December 16, 2019. arxiv .org/abs/1912.07726.

23. Cameron, Dell. "Detroit Police Chief Admits Face Recognition Doesn't Work '95–97% of the Time.'" Gizmodo, June 29, 2020. gizmodo.com/detroit -police-chief-admits-face-recognition-doesnt-wor-1844209113.

24. Bell, Lee. "What Is Moore's Law? Wired Explains the Theory That Defined the Tech Industry." *Wired* UK edition, August 28, 2016. wired.co .uk/article/wired-explains-moores-law.

Chapter Six: The Incredible Story of AlphaGo

25. *AlphaGo*. Greg Kohs, Director. RO*CO Films. Full documentary available on YouTube at youtube.com/watch?v=WXuK6gekU1Y.

Chapter Seven: But Can AI Be Clever?

26. 85,000 watts, compared with the 20 watts your body takes to power your brain.

27. Ferrucci, David, Eric Brown, et al. "The AI behind Watson." *AI Magazine*, Fall 2010. aaai.org/ai-magazine/the-ai-behind-watson-the-technical-article/.

28. Jennings, Ken. "Watson, *Jeopardy!* and Me, the Obsolete Know-It-All." TED Talk, TEDxSeattleU, February 2013. ted.com/talks/ken_jennings _watson_jeopardy_and_me_the_obsolete_know_it_all/transcript.

29. Markoff, John. "Computer Wins on 'Jeopardy!': Trivial, It's Not." *The New York Times*, February 16, 2011. nytimes.com/2011/02/17/science/17jeopardy-watson.html.

30. Kelly, John E. "Computing, Cognition and the Future of Knowing: How Humans and Machines Are Forging a New Age of Understanding." IBM, 2015. publicservicesalliance.org/wp-content/uploads/2015/10/Computing_Cognition_WhitePaper.pdf.

31. Lohr, Steve. "What Ever Happened to IBM's Watson?" *The New York Times*, July 16, 2021. nytimes.com/2021/07/16/technology/what-happened-ibm-watson.html.

Part II: The Quest for Thinking Machines

32. Liversidge, Anthony. "Interview with Claude Shannon." *Omni*, August 1987.

Chapter Eight: Brain Vs. Brain

33. Bellmund, Jacob L., Peter Gärdenfors, et al. "Navigating Cognition: Spatial Codes for Human Thinking." *Science*, 2018.

34. When my daughter was in middle school, one of her classmates lined the students up in order of clamminess. This is also a sort of mental mapping.

35. Koren, Marina. "B. F. Skinner: The Man Who Taught Pigeons to Play Ping-Pong and Rats to Pull Levers." Smithsonian.com, March 20, 2013. smithsonianmag.com/science-nature/bf-skinner-the-man-who-taught-pigeons-to-play-ping-pong-and-rats-to-pull-levers-5363946/.

36. Epstein, Robert. "Drs. Robert Epstein and B. F. Skinner with Pigeons, Part 1." A Research Press Production, Originally released 1982, Uploaded September 28, 2010. youtube.com/watch?v=QKSvu3mj-14.

37. Goodfellow, Ian, Yoshua Bengio, and Aaron Courville. *Deep Learning*. Cambridge, MA: MIT Press, 2016.

Chapter Nine: AI Is like a Sandwich

38. Lewis, Tanya. "What's the Universe Made of? Math, Says Scientist." LiveScience, January 30, 2014. livescience.com/42839-the-universe-is-math .html.

39. Kowalski, Kathiann. "Explainer: Correlation, Causation, Coincidence and More." Science News Explores, July 24, 2015. snexplores.org/article /explainer-correlation-causation-coincidence-and-more.

Chapter Ten: The Trouble with Pure Logic

40. "PancAIke Day and Machine Learning." Monolith AI Blog. monolithai.com/post/pancaike-day-and-machine-learning.

Chapter Eleven: Can AI Read Your Mind?

41. Elhaouij, Neska. "Project Overview: Emotion Navigation." MIT Media Lab, n.d. media.mit.edu/projects/emotional-navigation-system/overview/.

42. Fix, Juliet. "How Anxiety Scrambles Your Brain and Makes It Hard to Learn." *The Guardian*, November 21, 2015. theguardian.com/education /2015/nov/21/how-anxiety-scrambles-your-brain-and-makes-it-hard-to-learn.

43. Diaz, Jesus. "AI Is Learning How to Make You Cry at the Movies." Fast Company, December 12, 2017. fastcompany.com/90154101/ai-is -learning-how-to-make-you-cry-at-the-movies.

44. Preto, Sara. "Emotion-Reading Algorithms Cannot Predict Intentions via Facial Expressions." *USC News*, September 4, 2019. news.usc.edu /160360/algorithms-emotions-facial-expressions-predict-intentions/.

Part III: The Future Has Arrived

45. Ng, Andrew. "What AI Can and Can't Do." *Harvard Business Review*, September 21, 2017. https://hbr.org/2016/11/what-artificial-intelligence-can -and-cant-do-right-now.

Chapter Twelve: AI in the World Today

46. Brown, Lydia X. Z. "Tenant Screening Algorithms Enable Racial and Disability Discrimination at Scale, and Contribute to Broader Patterns of Injustice." Center for Democracy and Technology, July 7, 2021. cdt.org/insights/tenant-screening-algorithms-enable-racial-and-disability-discrimination-at-scale-and-contribute-to-broader-patterns-of-injustice/.

47. Capps, Kriston. "Landlords Are Using Next-Generation Eviction Tech." Bloomberg.com, February 26, 2020. bloomberg.com/news/articles/2020-02-26/landlords-are-using-next-generation-eviction-tech.

48. Brown, Lydia X. Z. "What Happens When Computer Programs Automatically Cut Benefits That Disabled People Rely on to Survive." Center for Democracy and Technology, October 21, 2020. cdt.org/insights/what-happens-when-computer-programs-automatically-cut-benefits-that-disabled-people-rely-on-to-survive/.

49. Metz, Cade. "Can A.I. Grade Your Next Test?" *The New York Times*, July 20, 2021. nytimes.com/2021/07/20/technology/ai-education-neural-networks.html.

50. Hill, Kashmir. "Accused of Cheating by an Algorithm, and a Professor She Had Never Met." *The New York Times*, May 27, 2022. nytimes.com/2022/05/27/technology/college-students-cheating-software-honorlock.html.

51. Cox, Tracy, for Penn State. "How Many People Get 'Long COVID'? More Than Half, Researchers Find." ScienceDaily, October 13, 2021. sciencedaily.com/releases/2021/10/211013114112.htm.

52. "CDC COVID Data Tracker." Centers for Disease Control and Prevention. Centers for Disease Control and Prevention, n.d. covid.cdc.gov/covid-data-tracker/#vaccination-states-jurisdictions.

53. Miller, Katharine. "AI for Predicting COVID-19 Prognosis." Stanford HAI, June 10, 2021. hai.stanford.edu/news/ai-predicting-covid-19-prognosis.

54. Xu, Q., X. Zhan, et al. "AI-Based Analysis of CT Images for Rapid

Triage of COVID-19 Patients." *NPJ Digital Medicine*, April 22, 2021. doi .org/10.1038/s41746-021-00446-z.

55. Kiefer, Julie. "AI Quickly Identifies Genetic Causes of Disease in Newborns." @theU, University of Utah, October 14, 2021. attheu .utah.edu/facultystaff/ai-technology-identifies-genetic-causes-of-serious -disease/.

56. Security.org Team. "2023 Credit Card Fraud Report." Security.org, January 31, 2023. security.org/digital-safety/credit-card-fraud-report/.

57. Spice, Byron. "Collision-Detecting Suitcase, Wayfinding App Help Blind People Navigate Airports." *Carnegie Mellon University News*, May 7, 2019. cmu.edu/news/stories/archives/2019/may/suitcase-helps-navigate -airports.html.

58. Tan, Haobin, Chang Chin, et al. "Flying Guide Dog: Walkable Path Discovery for the Visually Impaired Utilizing Drones and Transformer-Based Semantic Segmentation." arXiv, hosted by Cornell University, August 16, 2021. arxiv.org/pdf/2108.07007.pdf.

59. NASA. "The Causes of Climate Change." NASA Science. climate.nasa .gov/causes/.

60. Davenport, Frances V., and Noah S. Diffenbaugh. "Using Machine Learning to Analyze Physical Causes of Climate Change: A Case Study of U.S. Midwest Extreme Precipitation." *Geophysical Research Letters*, August 2021. agupubs.onlinelibrary.wiley.com/doi/10.1029/2021GL093787.

61. Markus, Frank. "How Artificial Intelligence Is Cutting Wait Time at Red Lights." *Motor Trend*, May 28, 2021. motortrend.com/features/traffic -control-system-red-lights-artificial-intelligence-ai/.

Chapter Thirteen: It Knows When You Are Sleeping

62. Stevens, Nikki, and Os Keyes. "Seeing Infrastructure: Race, Facial Recognition and the Politics of Data." *Cultural Studies*, March 26, 2021, pp. 833–853. doi.org/10.1080/09502386.2021.1895252.

63. Najibi, Alex. "Racial Discrimination in Face Recognition Technology."

Harvard University Graduate School of Arts and Sciences, Science in the News Blog, October 24, 2020. sitn.hms.harvard.edu/flash/2020/racial -discrimination-in-face-recognition-technology/.

64. Dave, Paresh, and Jeffrey Dastin. "Exclusive: Ukraine Has Started Using Clearview AI's Facial Recognition During War." Reuters, March 14, 2022. reuters.com/technology/exclusive-ukraine-has-started-using -clearview-ais-facial-recognition-during-war-2022-03-13/.

65. Hill, Kashmir. "What We Learned about Clearview AI and Its Secret 'Co-Founder.'" *The New York Times*, March 18, 2021. nytimes .com/2021/03/18/technology/clearview-facial-recognition-ai.html.

66. Richardson, Megan, Mark Andrejevic, and Jake Goldenfein. "Clearview AI Facial Recognition Breaches Australian Law." CHOICE, June 22, 2022. choice.com.au/consumers-and-data/protecting-your-data /data-laws-and-regulation/articles/clearview-ai-and-privacy-law.

Mac, Ryan. "Clearview AI, a Facial Recognition Company, Is Fined for Breach of Britain's Privacy Laws." *The New York Times*, November 29, 2021. nytimes.com/2021/11/29/technology/clearview-ai-uk-privacy-fine.html.

67. Pesenti, Jerome. "An Update on Our Use of Face Recognition." Meta website, About page, November 2, 2021. about.fb.com/news/2021/11 /update-on-use-of-face-recognition/.

68. Sullivan, Gail. "Cornell Ethics Board Did Not Pre-Approve Facebook Mood Manipulation Study." *The Washington Post*, July 1, 2014. washingtonpost.com/news/morning-mix/wp/2014/07/01/facebooks -emotional-manipulation-study-was-even-worse-than-you-thought/.

69. Guariglia, Matthew. "Geofence Warrants and Reverse Keyword Warrants Are So Invasive, Even Big Tech Wants to Ban Them." Electronic Frontier Foundation, May 13, 2022. eff.org/deeplinks/2022/05/geofence -warrants-and-reverse-keyword-warrants-are-so-invasive-even-big-tech -wants.

70. Day, Matt. "Amazon Alexa Data Could Be Accessed by 30,000 Employees, FTC Says." *Bloomberg.com*, June 1, 2023. bloomberg.com/news

/articles/2023-06-01/thirty-thousand-amazon-workers-could-access-alexa
-data-ftc-says.

71. Korolova, Aleksandra. "Facebook's Illusion of Control over Location-Related Ad Targeting." Medium, December 18, 2018. medium.com /@korolova/facebooks-illusion-of-control-over-location-related-ad-targeting -de7f865aee78.

72. Associated Press. "Facebook to Axe 'Discriminatory' Algorithm in US Government Settlement." *The Guardian*, June 21, 2022. theguardian.com /technology/2022/jun/21/facebook-lawsuit-settlement-advertising-lookalike -audience-doj.

73. Graham, Jefferson. "Check Your Settings If You Don't Want Google Tracking Every Move." *USA Today*, June 28, 2019. usatoday.com/story /tech/talkingtech/2019/06/24/change-settings-google-could-follow-you -even-no-app-opened/1434180001/.

74. Hall, Madison, Skye Gould, et al. "At Least 1,003 People Have Been Charged in the Capitol Insurrection So Far. This Searchable Table Shows Them All." Insider, February 16, 2023. insider.com/all-the-us-capitol-pro -trump-riot-arrests-charges-names-2021-1.

75. Warzel, Charlie, and Stuart A. Thompson. "They Stormed the Capitol. Their Apps Tracked Them." *The New York Times*, February 5, 2021. nytimes.com/2021/02/05/opinion/capitol-attack-cellphone-data.html.

Chapter Fourteen: Will You Have to Get a Driver's License?

76. Treviranus, Jutta. "Sidewalk Toronto and Why Smarter Is Not Better.*" Medium, reprinted from DataDrivenInvestor, October 30, 2018. medium.datadriveninvestor.com/sidewalk-toronto-and-why-smarter-is-not -better-b233058d01c8.

77. Krisher, Tom, and Stefanie Dazio. "Felony Charges Are 1st in a Fatal Crash Involving Autopilot." Associated Press, January 18, 2022. apnews .com/article/tesla-autopilot-fatal-crash-charges-91b4a0341e07244f3f03051b 5c2462ae.

78. Cusack, Jenny. "How Driverless Cars Will Change Our World." BBC Future, November 29, 2021. bbc.com/future/article/20211126-how-driverless-cars-will-change-our-world.

79. Eisenstein, Paul A. "Millions of Professional Drivers Will Be Replaced by Self-Driving Vehicles." NBCNews.com, November 5, 2017. nbcnews.com/business/autos/millions-professional-drivers-will-be-replaced-self-driving-vehicles-n817356.

80. Clevenger, Seth. "Embark Self-Driving Truck Completes Coast-to-Coast Test Run." Transport Topics, February 6, 2018. ttnews.com/articles/embark-self-driving-truck-completes-coast-coast-test-run.

81. Rodrigues, Alex, Richard Hawwa, and Ian Robertson. "Investor Presentation June 2021." Embark website. embarktrucks.com/wp-content/uploads/2021/09/Embark_NGAB_Investor_Presentation.pdf.

Chapter Fifteen: The Trouble with Bots

82. Christian, Brian. "The Samantha Test." *The New Yorker*, December 30, 2013. newyorker.com/culture/culture-desk/the-samantha-test.

83. Metz, Cade. "Riding out Quarantine with a Chatbot Friend: 'I Feel Very Connected.'" *The New York Times*, June 16, 2020. nytimes.com/2020/06/16/technology/chatbots-quarantine-coronavirus.html.

84. Bardhan, Ashley. "Men Are Creating AI Girlfriends and Then Verbally Abusing Them," *Futurism*, January 18, 2022. futurism.com/chatbot-abuse.

85. Adaptive Agents Group. "The Shibboleth Rule for Artificial Agents." Stanford University Human-Centered Artificial Intelligence, August 10, 2021. hai.stanford.edu/news/shibboleth-rule-artificial-agents.

86. Ibid.

87. Schneier, Bruce. "Bots Are Destroying Political Discourse as We Know It." *The Atlantic*, January 7, 2020. theatlantic.com/technology/archive/2020/01/future-politics-bots-drowning-out-humans/604489/.

88. Stocking, Galen, and Nami Sumida. "Social Media Bots Draw Public's Attention and Concern." Pew Research Center's Journalism Project,

October 15, 2018. pewresearch.org/journalism/2018/10/15/social-media
-bots-draw-publics-attention-and-concern/.

89. Yang, Kai-Cheng, Onur Varol, et al. "Arming the Public with Artificial
Intelligence to Counter Social Bots." arXiv, hosted by Cornell University,
February 6, 2019. arxiv.org/pdf/1901.00912.pdf.

90. Ienca, Marcello, and Effy Vayena. "Cambridge Analytica and Online
Manipulation." Scientific American Blog Network, March 30, 2018. blogs
.scientificamerican.com/observations/cambridge-analytica-and-online
-manipulation/.

91. Kahn, Jeffrey P., Effy Vanena, and Anna C. Mastroianni. "Opinion:
Learning as We Go: Lessons from the Publication of Facebook's Social-
Computing Research." *Proceedings of the National Academy of Sciences*,
September 23, 2014. pnas.org/doi/pdf/10.1073/pnas.1416405111.

92. Mayer, Jane. "New Evidence Emerges of Steve Bannon and Cambridge
Analytica's Role in Brexit." *The New Yorker*, November 17, 2018.
newyorker.com/news/news-desk/new-evidence-emerges-of-steve-bannon
-and-cambridge-analyticas-role-in-brexit.

93. Schwartz, Brian. "Mercer Family Played Bigger Role in 2020 Election
Than Thought, Giving Nearly $20 Million to Dark Money GOP Fund."
CNBC, September 15, 2021. cnbc.com/2021/09/15/robert-mercer-family
-gave-nearly-20-million-to-dark-money-gop-fund-during-2020-election
.html.

94. I worked at Microsoft, where stereotypes about people were not
only rampant, products were designed around them. The personas often
sounded like this: "Julie is a 35-year-old mom of three who listens to NPR
and shops at Trader Joe's."

95. Choon, Chang May. "Controversy over AI Chatbot in South Korea
Raises Questions About Ethics, Data Collection." *The Straits Times*,
January 23, 2021. straitstimes.com/asia/east-asia/controversy-over-ai
-chatbot-in-south-korea-raises-questions-about-ethics-data.

Chapter Sixteen: A Machine with a Soul?

96. Sisto, Davide. "Chatting with the Dead." The MIT Press Reader, January 4, 2021. thereader.mitpress.mit.edu/chatting-with-the-dead -chatbots/.

97. Ibid.

98. Fagone, Jason. "The Jessica Simulation: Love and Loss in the Age of AI." *The San Francisco Chronicle*, July 23, 2021. sfchronicle.com/projects /2021/jessica-simulation-artificial-intelligence/.

99. Tiku, Nitasha. "The Google Engineer Who Thinks the Company's AI Has Come to Life." *The Washington Post*, June 11, 2022. washingtonpost .com/technology/2022/06/11/google-ai-lamda-blake-lemoine/.

100. Lemoine, Blake. "Is LaMDA Sentient? An Interview." DocumentCloud, accessed June 28, 2022. documentcloud.org/documents /22058315-is-lamda-sentient-an-interview, p. 8.

101. Ibid., pp. 5–6.

Part IV: What's Next with AI

102. Kurzweil, Raymond. "Kurzweil: Tracking the Acceleration of Intelligence," KurzweilAI.net, March 14, 2017. futurism.com/kurzweil -claims-that-the-singularity-will-happen-by-2045.

Chapter Seventeen: AI and Global Competition

103. Young, Jabari. "Super Bowl 2022 Attracted More Than 112 Million Viewers, but Failed to Top Record." CNBC, February 15, 2022. cnbc .com/2022/02/15/super-bowl-2022-ratings-.html.

104. Hvistendahl, Mara. "Inside China's Vast New Experiment in Social Ranking." *Wired*, December 14, 2017. wired.com/story/age-of-social-credit/.

105. Song, Bing. "Opinion: The West May Be Wrong About China's Social Credit System." *The Washington Post*, November 29, 2018. washingtonpost.com/news/theworldpost/wp/2018/11/29/social-credit/.

106. Kuo, Lily. "China Bans 23m from Buying Travel Tickets as Part of

'Social Credit' System." *The Guardian*, March 1, 2019. theguardian.com
/world/2019/mar/01/china-bans-23m-discredited-citizens-from-buying
-travel-tickets-social-credit-system.

107. Lee, Kai-Fu. *AI Superpowers: China, Silicon Valley, and the New World
Order.* New York: Houghton Mifflin Harcourt, 2018, pp. 23–25.

108. Martinez, A. "FBI Says China Could Use TikTok to Spy on
Americans, Including Government Workers." NPR, November 16, 2022.
npr.org/2022/11/16/1137076864/fbi-says-china-could-use-tiktok-to-spy-on
-americans-including-government-workers.

109. Sherman, Priscilla. "The Privacy Risks of TikTok: Why This Invasive
App Is So Dangerous." VPNOverview, January 26, 2023. vpnoverview
.com/privacy/social-media/tiktok-privacy/.

110. Council on Foreign Relations. "Assessing China's Digital Silk Road:
A Transformative Approach to Technology Financing or a Danger to
Freedoms?" Council on Foreign Relations, accessed May 16, 2022. cfr.org
/china-digital-silk-road/.

111. Peterson, Dahlia. "Designing Alternatives to China's Repressive
Surveillance State: CSET Policy Brief." Center for Security and Emerging
Technology, Georgetown University, October 2020. cset.georgetown.edu
/wp-content/uploads/CSET-Designing-Alternatives-to-Chinas-Surveillance
-State.pdf.

Chapter Eighteen: Warfare and National Security

112. Katz, Brian. "The Analytic Edge: Leveraging Emerging Technologies
to Transform Intelligence Analysis." Center for Strategic and International
Studies, October 9, 2020. csis.org/analysis/analytic-edge-leveraging
-emerging-technologies-transform-intelligence-analysis.

113. Andrews, Edmund L. "Re-Imagining Espionage in the Era of
Artificial Intelligence." Stanford Institute for Human-Centered Artificial
Intelligence, August 17, 2021. hai.stanford.edu/news/re-imagining
-espionage-era-artificial-intelligence.

114. Gambrell, Jon. "Analysts: Fire at Iran Nuclear Site Hit
Centrifuge Facility." Associated Press, July 2, 2020. apnews.com/article
/50c3e7f6445ae99def6bdc65fbce6c42.

115. Office of the United States Trade Representative Staff. "The People's
Republic of China: US-China Trade Facts." Office of the United States
Trade Representative, 2020. ustr.gov/countries-regions/china-mongolia
-taiwan/peoples-republic-china.

116. Perlo-Freeman, Sam. "Arms Race." Britannica. britannica.com/topic
/arms-race.

117. Jing, Yuan-Chou. "How Does China Aim to Use AI in Warfare?" *The
Diplomat*, December 28, 2021. thediplomat.com/2021/12/how-does-china
-aim-to-use-ai-in-warfare/.

118. Ibid.

119. Simonite, Tom. "A Zelensky Deepfake Was Quickly Defeated.
The next One Might Not Be." *Wired*, March 17, 2022. wired.com/story
/zelensky-deepfake-facebook-twitter-playbook/.

120. Ecker, Ullrich K. H., Stephan Lewandowsky, et al. "The
Psychological Drivers of Misinformation Belief and Its Resistance to
Correction." *Nature Reviews Psychology*, January 12, 2022, pp. 13–29.
doi.org/10.1038/s44159-021-00006-y.

121. Internet Crime Complaint Center (IC3). "Public Service
Announcement: Deepfakes and Stolen PII Utilized to Apply for Remote
Work Positions." Federal Bureau of Investigation, June 28, 2022. ic3.gov
/Media/Y2022/PSA220628.

122. Freedberg, Sydney J., Jr. "Robot Wars: Centaurs, Skynet, & Swarms."
Breaking Defense, December 31, 2015. breakingdefense.com/2015/12/robot
-wars-centaurs-skynet-swarms/.

123. Gall, Carlotta. "On the Trail of Russian War Crimes." *The New York
Times*, April 29, 2022. nytimes.com/2022/04/29/world/europe/on-the-trail
-of-russian-war-crimes.html.

124. Freedberg, "Robot Wars: Centaurs, Skynet, & Swarms."

125. Hernandez, Joe. "A Military Drone with a Mind of Its Own Was Used in Combat, U.N. Says." NPR, June 1, 2021. npr.org/2021/06/01 /1002196245/a-u-n-report-suggests-libya-saw-the-first-battlefield-killing-by -an-autonomous-d.

Chapter Nineteen: Will AI Take My Job?

126. Lee, *AI Superpowers*, p. 157.

127. This is a nonalcoholic cocktail made with 7UP, grenadine syrup, and a maraschino cherry. A Roy Rogers is made using Coca-Cola instead of 7UP.

128. Wallis, Lucy. "Servants: A Life Below Stairs." BBC News, September 21, 2012. bbc.com/news/magazine-19544309.

129. Eloundou, Tyna, Sam Manning, et al. "GPTs Are GPTs: An Early Look at the Labor Market Impact Potential of Large Language Models." arXiv, hosted by Cornell University, March 23, 2023. arxiv.org/abs/2303.10130.

130. Grace, Katja, John Salvatier, et al., "When Will AI Exceed Human Performance? Evidence from AI Experts." arXiv, hosted by Cornell University, May 3, 2018. arxiv.org/pdf/1705.08807.pdf.

131. Treisman, Rachel. "California Program Giving $500 No-Strings-Attached Stipends Pays Off, Study Finds." NPR, March 4, 2021. npr.org/2021/03/04/973653719/california-program-giving-500-no-strings -attached-stipends-pays-off-study-finds.

132. Experts debate exactly how long ago. There's some evidence of farming in the Middle East 23,000 years ago.

American Friends of Tel Aviv University. "First Evidence of Farming in Mideast 23,000 Years Ago: Evidence of Earliest Small-Scale Agricultural Cultivation." ScienceDaily, July 22, 2015. sciencedaily.com /releases/2015/07/150722144709.htm.

133. Vaughn, Mark. "Autonomous Tractors with Robot Brains Are Coming to Take Over the Farm." *Autoweek*, January 12, 2022. autoweek .com/news/future-cars/a38705415/autonomous-tractors-robot-brains-for -farming/.

134. Revanth. "Towards Future Farming: How Artificial Intelligence Is Transforming the Agriculture Industry." Wipro, November 2019. wipro.com/holmes/towards-future-farming-how-artificial-intelligence-is-transforming-the-agriculture-industry/.

135. Expo 2020 Staff. "The Voice of the Pavilion." Expo 2020 Dubai UAE, accessed November 16, 2022. events.great.gov.uk/website/3127/algorithm/.

136. AIArtists.org. "Timeline of AI Art." 2021. aiartists.org/ai-timeline-art.

137. "Is Artificial Intelligence Set to Become Art's Next Medium?" Christies, December 12, 2018. christies.com/features/a-collaboration-between-two-artists-one-human-one-a-machine-9332-1.aspx.

Chapter Twenty: AI and Your Body

138. Also known as the GDP, the gross domestic product represents the value of all goods and services produced in a country. The US and China have the highest GDPs in the world.

139. Ireland, Sophie. "Revealed: Countries with the Best Health Care Systems, 2021." *Ceoworld Magazine*, April 27, 2021. ceoworld.biz/2021/04/27/revealed-countries-with-the-best-health-care-systems-2021/.

140. Schneider, Eric C., Arnav Shah, et al., "Mirror, Mirror 2021: Reflecting Poorly." Commonwealth Fund, August 4, 2021. commonwealthfund.org/publications/fund-reports/2021/aug/mirror-mirror-2021-reflecting-poorly.

141. Tikkanen, Roosa, Robin Osborn, et al. "International Health Care System Profiles: United States." The Commonwealth Fund, June 5, 2020. commonwealthfund.org/international-health-policy-center/countries/united-states.

142. Kirby, Philip. "Dyslexia Debated, Then and Now: A Historical Perspective on the Dyslexia Debate." *Oxford Review of Education*, August 13, 2020. ncbi.nlm.nih.gov/pmc/articles/PMC7455059/.

143. Centers for Disease Control and Prevention. "Heart Disease Facts."

Centers for Disease Control and Prevention, February 7, 2022. cdc.gov /heartdisease/facts.htm.

144. Cunningham, Mary, and George Mason University. "AI Can Predict Probability of COVID-19 vs. Flu Based on Symptoms." ScienceDaily, April 13, 2022. sciencedaily.com/releases/2022/04/220412161553.htm.

145. Cohut, Maria. "Are Dogs Better at Detecting Cancer 'than Advanced Technology?'" Medical News Today, June 19, 2019. medicalnewstoday.com /articles/325511.

146. Elliker, Kevin R., Barbara A. Sommerville, et al. "Key Considerations for the Experimental Training and Evaluation of Cancer Odour Detection Dogs: Lessons Learnt from a Double-Blind, Controlled Trial of Prostate Cancer Detection." *BMC Urology*, February 27, 2014. ncbi.nlm.nih.gov /pmc/articles/PMC3945616/.

147. Coolbrandt, Stijn. "How AI Will Keep You Healthy." Medium, published in Tincture, March 4, 2017. tincture.io/how-ai-will-keep-you -healthy-7140a78e18aa.

148. Larsen, Rasmus Tolstrup, Vibeke Wagner, et al. "Effectiveness of Physical Activity Monitors in Adults: Systematic Review and Meta-Analysis." *BMJ*, January 26, 2022. bmj.com/content/376/bmj-2021-068047.

149. Mishra, Tejaswini, Meng Wang, et al. "Pre-Symptomatic Detection of Covid-19 from Smartwatch Data." *Nature Biomedical Engineering*, November 18, 2020. nature.com/articles/s41551-020-00640-6.

150. Chankova, Slavea. "Wearable Devices Are Connecting Health Care to Daily Life." *The Economist*, May 2, 2022. economist.com/technology -quarterly/2022/05/02/wearable-devices-are-connecting-health-care-to -daily-life.

151. Dhunnoo, Pranavsingh. "The Future of Prosthetics Depends on A.I." The Medical Futurist, September 1, 2020. medicalfuturist.com/the-future -of-prosthetics-depends-on-a-i/.

152. Ibid.

153. National Institutes of Health. "Fact Sheet: Artificial Intelligence,

Machine Learning and Genomics." National Human Genome Research Institute, January 12, 2022. genome.gov/about-genomics/educational -resources/fact-sheets/artificial-intelligence-machine-learning-and-genomics.

154. Johns Hopkins University. "Robot Performs First Laparoscopic Surgery Without Human Help." ScienceDaily, January 26, 2022. sciencedaily.com/releases/2022/01/220126143954.htm.

155. Chidambaram, Priya. "Over 200,000 Residents and Staff in Long-Term Care Facilities Have Died from COVID-19." Kaiser Family Foundation, February 3, 2022. kff.org/policy-watch/over-200000-residents -and-staff-in-long-term-care-facilities-have-died-from-covid-19/.

156. Leland, John. "Can Robots Save Nursing Homes?" *The New York Times*, April 21, 2022. nytimes.com/2022/04/21/realestate/nursing-home -robots.html.

157. PARO Robots USA website. parorobots.com/.

158. Leland, "Can Robots Save Nursing Homes?"

Chapter Twenty-One: All's Fair in Love

159. Marriage over the ages has taken many forms, not just pairs.
   Editors of Encyclopaedia Britannica. "Marriage." *Britannica*, April 11, 2022. britannica.com/topic/marriage.

160. Dooley, Ben, and Hisako Ueno. "This Man Married a Fictional Character. He'd Like You to Hear Him Out." *The New York Times*, April 24, 2022. nytimes.com/2022/04/24/business/akihiko-kondo-fictional -character-relationships.html.

161. Aron, Arthur, Helen Fisher, et al. "Reward, Motivation, and Emotion Systems Associated with Early-Stage Intense Romantic Love." *Journal of Neurophysiology*, July 1, 2005. journals.physiology.org/doi/full/10.1152 /jn.00838.2004.

162. Zhang, Xiaochu, Zhiling Zou, and Andreas J. Fallgatter. "Editorial: Beyond Reward: Insights from Love and Addiction." *Frontiers in Psychology*, November 15, 2016. ncbi.nlm.nih.gov/pmc/articles/PMC5108782/.

163. Laslocky, Meghan. "This Is Your Brain on Heartbreak." Greater Good, February 15, 2013. greatergood.berkeley.edu/article/item/this_is _your_brain_on_heartbreak.

164. Nader, Karim. "Dating Through the Filters." *Social Philosophy and Policy*, Winter 2020, pp. 237–248. cambridge.org/core/journals/social -philosophy-and-policy/article/dating-through-the-filters/EA64BE27CD7D2 A1749D712A5E179828D.

165. Ma, Zilin, and Krzysztof Z. Gajos. "Not Just a Preference: Reducing Biased Decision-Making on Dating Websites." *Proceedings of the 2022 CHI Conference on Human Factors in Computing Systems*, April 2022. doi.org/10 .1145/3491102.3517587.

Chapter Twenty-Two: How Do You Know If AI Is Alive?

166. Zimmer, Carl. *Life's Edge: The Search for What It Means to Be Alive*. New York, NY: Dutton, 2021, p. 234.

167. Galeon, Dom. "Google's Artificial Intelligence Built an AI That Outperforms Any Made by Humans." Futurism, December 1, 2017. futurism.com/google-artificial-intelligence-built-ai.

168. Descartes, René. "Discourse on Method." trans. John Cottingham, Robert Stoothoff, Dugald Murdoch. *The Philosophical Works of Descartes. Volume I*, Cambridge: Cambridge University Press, 1984.

169. Rowell, Misha K., Neville Pillay, and Tasmin L. Rymer. "Problem Solving in Animals: Proposal for an Ontogenetic Perspective." *Animals*, March 18, 2021. ncbi.nlm.nih.gov/pmc/articles/PMC8002912/.

170. Many years ago, when I was a young newspaper reporter, I was assigned to cover the birth of a beluga whale at the Point Defiance Zoo and Aquarium in Tacoma, Washington. The baby was born alive—and then drowned. Its grieving mother carried its placenta on her head for days.

171. Mori, Masahiro, Karl F. MacDorman, and Norri Kageki. "The Uncanny Valley." *IEEE Robots and Automation Magazine*, June 2012, pp. 98–100. ieeexplore.ieee.org/document/6213238.

172. Schneider, Susan, and Edwin Turner. "Is Anyone Home? A Way to Find Out If AI Has Become Self-Aware." Scientific American Blog Network, July 19, 2017. blogs.scientificamerican.com/observations/is -anyone-home-a-way-to-find-out-if-ai-has-become-self-aware/.

Chapter Twenty-Three: Making AI Safe

173. Snapes, Laura. "Taylor Swift Used Facial Recognition Software to Detect Stalkers at LA Concert." *The Guardian*, December 13, 2018. theguardian.com/music/2018/dec/13/taylor-swift-facial-recognition-stalkers -rose-bowl-concert.

174. Ng, Alfred. "With Facial Recognition, Shoplifting May Get You Banned in Places You've Never Been." CNET, March 20, 2019. cnet.com /news/privacy/with-facial-recognition-shoplifting-may-get-you-banned-in -places-youve-never-been/.

175. Lin, Bai. "Public Pajamas Persist in Shanghai." *The Wall Street Journal*, October 29, 2009. wsj.com/articles/BL-CJB-4986.

176. Council on Foreign Relations. "Assessing China's Digital Silk Road Initiative."

177. Statista. "Number of TikTok Users in the United States from 2019 to 2025." Statista. statista.com/statistics/1100836/number-of-us-tiktok-users/.

178. Leonard, Bill. "Study Suggests Bias Against 'Black' Names on Resumes." SHRM, February 1, 2003. shrm.org/hr-today/news/hr-magazine /pages/0203hrnews2.aspx.

179. Funk, Cary, and Kim Parker. "Women in STEM See More Gender Disparities at Work, Especially Those in Computer Jobs, Majority-Male Workplaces." *Women and Men in STEM Often at Odds over Workplace Equity*. Pew Research Center, December 31, 2019. pewresearch.org/social -trends/2018/01/09/women-in-stem-see-more-gender-disparities-at-work -especially-those-in-computer-jobs-majority-male-workplaces/.

180. A housing shortage in 1933 prompted the US government to create a program to increase America's housing stock. This New Deal program

provided housing to white families in the lower and middle classes. People of color were excluded from these new suburban areas and corralled into urban housing projects. In 1934, the government established the Federal Housing Administration. The FHA wouldn't insure mortgages in Black neighborhoods, but they paid back builders who created suburbs restricted to white people. For more about this, read Richard Rothstein's book *The Color of Law: A Forgotten History of How Our Government Segregated America* (W. W. Norton/Liveright, 2017).

181. Obermeyer, Ziad, Brian Powers, et al. "Dissecting Racial Bias in an Algorithm Used to Manage the Health of Populations." *Science*, October 25, 2019, pp. 447–453.

182. Miller, Katharine. "IRS Disproportionately Audits Black Taxpayers." Stanford HAI, January 31, 2023. hai.stanford.edu/news/irs -disproportionately-audits-black-taxpayers.

183. Levin, Sam. "A Beauty Contest Was Judged by AI and the Robots Didn't Like Dark Skin." *The Guardian*, September 8, 2016. theguardian .com/technology/2016/sep/08/artificial-intelligence-beauty-contest-doesnt -like-black-people.

184. Buolamwini, Joy. "Artificial Intelligence Has a Problem with Gender and Racial Bias. Here's How to Solve It." *Time*, February 7, 2019. time.com /5520558/artificial-intelligence-racial-gender-bias/.

185. German, Michael. "Hidden in Plain Sight: Racism, White Supremacy, and Far-Right Militancy in Law Enforcement." Brennan Center for Justice, August 27, 2020. brennancenter.org/our-work/research-reports/hidden -plain-sight-racism-white-supremacy-and-far-right-militancy-law.

186. Lehr, Amy K., and Efthimia Maria Bechrakis. "The United States Blacklisted 28 Chinese Entities over Repression of Muslim Minorities in Xinjiang. What Does This Mean for Human Rights?" Center for Strategic and International Studies, October 11, 2019. csis.org/analysis/united-states -blacklisted-28-chinese-entities-over-repression-muslim-minorities-xinjiang.

187. Bolukbasi, Tolga, Kai-Wei Chang, et al. "Man Is to Computer

Programmer as Woman Is to Homemaker? Debiasing Word Embeddings."
arXiv, hosted by Cornell University, July 21, 2016. arxiv.org/abs/1607.06520.

188. Uzzi, Brian. "A Simple Tactic That Could Help Reduce Bias in AI."
Harvard Business Review, November 4, 2020. hbr.org/2020/11/a-simple
-tactic-that-could-help-reduce-bias-in-ai.

189. Osaka University. "Machine Learning Writes Songs That Elicits
Emotions from Its Listeners." ScienceDaily, March 9, 2017. sciencedaily
.com/releases/2017/03/170309120651.htm.

190. Salge, Christoph, and Daniel Polani. "Empowerment as Replacement
for the Three Laws of Robotics." Frontiers, June 29, 2017. frontiersin.org
/articles/10.3389/frobt.2017.00025/full.

191. To ask Delphi your own question, go to delphi.allenai.org.

Acknowledgments

This book took years to research and write, and I am grateful for everyone who stood by me during that time. My family—especially Adam, Lucy, and Alice—as well as my agent, Jennifer Laughran, my editor, Kat Brzozowski, and the inimitable Jean Feiwel.

I am a lucky author to keep such company.

Curious, I asked the chatbot known as ChatGPT how long this task *should* have taken. I was hoping it would make me feel better. Dear reader, it did not.

The time it takes to write a book about artificial intelligence for young readers depends on several factors, such as writing speed, research time, and level of detail. However, as a rough estimate, it could take anywhere from several months to a year or more to write a book of average length for this audience.

ChatGPT, which did not exist when I started my research, had missed something important. I had to say something.

Why didn't you factor in changing technology as part of this estimate?

You are correct, my previous answer did not take into account the fact that technology in the field of artificial intelligence is constantly evolving. This means that the amount of time it takes to write a book about AI for young readers may need to be longer to ensure that the information is up-to-date and accurate at the time of publication. Additionally, the author may need to invest more time in ongoing research and revision to keep the content current, which could further extend the writing process.

The emotional bond I'd formed with this bot started to veer into the red zone.

Why didn't you consider the fact that writers need to get feedback from friends on their books, to make sure everything is as accessible as possible?

Thank you for pointing that out. I apologize for the oversight. Getting feedback from friends, peers, or beta readers can be an important part of the writing process and can help ensure that the book is accessible and understandable for the intended audience. This can add additional time to the writing process as the author incorporates suggestions, makes revisions, and seeks further feedback. So, this is an important factor that should be taken into consideration when estimating the time it takes to write a book.

To that end, I am indebted to the following for their feedback: Jack Thompson, Elana K. Arnold, Jolie Stekly, Tom Doelger, Rebecca Kirshenbaum, JP McKormick, and a large group of others whose data I will keep secret. ChatGPT only wishes it had such a crew.

But it wasn't just that. I also worked with experts in the field to ensure the text was as accurate as possible. What did ChatGPT think about this?

Yes, obtaining feedback from experts in the field can be a responsible and important part of the writing process for a book about artificial intelligence, particularly for a book aimed at young readers. This can help ensure that the information presented is accurate and up-to-date and can also provide valuable insights and perspectives that the author may not have considered. However, like seeking feedback from friends and peers, this can also add time to the writing process as the author waits for and incorporates feedback from experts. It is important to balance the need for expert input with the need to meet deadlines and get the book to market in a timely manner.

Some of my professional reviewers will remain anonymous at their request, but I was fortunate to have the scholarly insights of Johnathan Flowers, Os Keyes, Guillermo Alexander, and Barbara Cohen. But even more people played invaluable roles.

Are you aware, ChatGPT, that books are also read by editors, copy editors, fact checkers, proofreaders, and designers, not to mention sales and marketing teams? And that their participation takes time?

Yes, I am aware that books often go through several stages of review and editing before they are published. This process typically includes review by editors, lawyers, copy editors, fact checkers, and proofreaders. These individuals play important roles in ensuring that the book is of high quality and ready for publication. The time required for these reviews and edits can vary depending on the complexity of the book, the size of the publisher, and other factors, but they are usually included in the overall timeline for getting a book to market.

Given all the work that goes into a book, and all the human beings required to do that work, do you still think this can be done in six months to a year?

ChatGPT was silent for a long time. And then this reply appeared, in red type:

An error occurred. If this issue persists please contact us through our help center at help.openai.com.

Yes, that's what I thought. It would break an AI to do the work that flesh-and-blood humans do every day to bring books like this to the world.

For however long the world still requires teams of us to do this, to answer the questions of young readers, to provide them with reliable information that they will need, and to fill them with wonder at the possibilities presented by being alive in this world, I am honored, thrilled, and overjoyed to persist.

Index

Note: Page references in *italics* indicate images.

with a soul," 141
Tay, 137
the very first, 128
virtual assistants, 132
Xiaoice, 137
ChatGPT, 176
Cheating, 99, 171
Checkers, 25, 30–31
Chefs, 176
Chess, 29–33, 171
Children, 105–6, 197–98
China
   AI-enhanced military strategy,
      159–60
   AI-powered chatbot, 137
   anti-Communist bots, 138
   cognitive warfare, 160
   data-gathering ability, 151–53
   Digital Silk Road, 154–55, 207
   driverless taxis in, 125
   facial recognition use, 211
   government funding of technology,
      151
   invention of Go, 41
   loan applications, 95
   People's Liberation Army, 159
   public investment in AI, 151
   social credit system, 151–52
   surveillance tools, 154–55, 206–7
   technology copycats, 152–53
   trade rivalry with US, 159
   -US relations, 149–55, 159
Chinook, 30–31
ChipTest, 32
A Christmas Carol (Dickens), 184
Circuits, 16
Citizens United v. FEC, 136
Classrooms, 89–90, 97–100
Clearview AI, 113–14
Climate change, 108–9
Clothing, sensor-embedded, 187
Coders, 171–72
Cognitive warfare, 160
Cold War, 150
College admissions, 96
Combat, automated, 164–66
Combat planes, 166

Communication, *18*
   over long distances, 17–20
   predictability of, 18–19
   redundancy in, 19
   role of emotions in, 86
   verbal and nonverbal, 87–88
Communist Party, 138, 149, 150
Computer chips, 39
Computerized essay graders, 98–99
Computers
   analog, 13–14
   architecture of, 17
   "human," 13
   increasing power of, 64–65
   primitive, 26
Consciousness, 6, 199–203
Convolutional, defined, 36
Cooks, 176
Copycat technology, 152–53
COVID-19, detecting, 186
COVID-19 pandemic, 100–104, 183,
      192–93
Credit cards, 106
Credit scores, 151
Cruise, Tom, *162*, 162–63
CT-scan images, 102
Cultural context, 79
Customer service, 134
Cyrano de Bergerac, 128

D
Dadbot, 140
Daily Doubles, 50–51
Damasio, Antonio, 85
Dark money, 136
Dartmouth summer conference, 25–26
Data
   from bad datasets, 104
   Benford's Law violations, 164
   gathered in China, 151–53
   generated by smartphones, 118–20
   generated by social media, 74
   helpful versus harmful, 138
   paying for, 179
Data-tracking apps, 152
Dating coaches, 197
Dating services, 196

Robots, *8*
  agricultural, 180–81
  baby, 198
  compared to AI, 3–4
  early forms of, 67–68
  kill-switch option, 215
  in nursing homes, 192–93
  pervasiveness of, 8
  Three Laws of Robotics, 213–14
  training failures, 80
Rodrigues, Alex, 126
Rohrer, Jason, 141
Rosenblatt, Frank, 26–27
Russia, 113–14, 161–62, 164–65, 166
Rutter, Brad, 52

S
Sales managers, 175
Samantha (bot), 141
Samuel, Arthur, 25, 30
Satellites, commercial, 157–58, *158*
Satellites, weather, 158
Scammers, 133
Schaeffer, Jonathan, 31
Schools
  AI in, 171
  AI in classrooms, 97–100
  anxious students, 89–90
  emotional support, 90
  teachers, 98, 100, 171
Science fiction writers, 212–13
Science Museum in London, 15
Search engines, 6–7
Security cameras, 205–6
Sedol, Lee, 44–46, *46*, 150
Self-driving cars, 122–25
Self-driving trucks, 126
Sensory skills, 62
Sentience, evidence of, 143–44
Service workers, 173
Shannon, Claude, 15–16, *16*, 17, 19, 25, 29, 30, 55
Shi, Yan, 9
Shoplifting, 205
Sight, in humans, 202
SimCity, 11
Simon, Herbert, 26

"The singularity," 64–65, 147
Skin cancers, 186
Skinner, B. F., 63, *63*
Slavery, 218
Smart, John, 40
Smartphones
  AI in, 4, 6
  in China, 152
  data generated by, 118–20
  data recorded by, 152
Social credit scores, 151–52
Social credit system, 151
Social media. *See also* Facebook; TikTok
  AI used on, 6, 7
  bots on, 133
  data generated by, 74
  facial recognition on, 111–12
  location tracking on, 116–17
  manipulation on, 134–35
  photos and videos uploaded to, 163
  TikTok, 4, 154, 162, 163, 207
Soft tissue surgeries, 190–91
Software industry, 172
Soldiers, automated, 165
Soldiers, pairing with AI, 166
Songwriting, 181
Southern, Taryn, 181
South Korea, 44, 138
Soviet Union, 150
"Spaces on wheels," 125
SpaceX, 157
Sportswriters, 170
Sputnik satellite, 150
Spy agencies, 156–57
Stanford, 98
STAR (Smart Tissue Autonomous Robot), 190–91, *191*
Stealth combat plane, 166
Stereotypes, 38
Stevie (robot), 193
Stress, detecting, 89
Students. *See* Schools
Suanpan, *10*
Suitcase, rolling, 107
Supervised learning, 42, 74–75
Surgeons, robotic, 190–91

Thank you for reading this Feiwel & Friends book. The friends
who made *Future Tense* possible are:

Jean Feiwel, Publisher
Liz Szabla, VP, Associate Publisher
Rich Deas, Senior Creative Director
Holly West, Senior Editor
Anna Roberto, Senior Editor
Kat Brzozowski, Senior Editor
Dawn Ryan, Executive Managing Editor
Kim Waymer, Senior Production Manager
Emily Settle, Editor
Rachel Diebel, Editor
Foyinsi Adegbonmire, Associate Editor
Brittany Groves, Assistant Editor
Mallory Grigg, Senior Art Director
Ellen Duda, Designer
Lelia Mander, Production Editor

Follow us on Facebook or visit us online at mackids.com. Our
books are friends for life.